George Orwell's
Commander in Spain

T0284537

George Orwell's Commander in Spain

The Enigma of Georges Kopp

Marc Wildemeersch

THAMES RIVER PRESS

George Orwell's Commander in Spain: The Enigma of Georges Kopp

THAMES RIVER PRESS
An imprint of Wimbledon Publishing Company Limited (WPC)
Another imprint of WPC is Anthem Press (www.anthempress.com)
First published in the United Kingdom in 2013 by
THAMES RIVER PRESS
75–76 Blackfriars Road
London SE1 8HA

www.thamesriverpress.com

Original title: *De man die Belg wilde worden: Georges Kopp,
commandant van George Orwell*
Copyright © Marc Wildemeersch 2010
Originally published in Haarlem by Uitgeverij In de Knipscheer
This extended and revised English edition © Marc Wildemeersch 2013

A CIP record for this book is available from the British Library.

ISBN 978-0-85728-198-2

This title is also available as an ebook.

'I've always felt – and without wishing to sound like Heidegger – that the business of consciousness and the business of life itself, and our spiralling apprehension of it, are more and more mysterious. As a consequence I've become increasingly preoccupied by what it means to make a conscientious statement about the world.'

– J. O'Neill, *Netherland*

TABLE OF CONTENTS

INTRODUCTION BY THE AUTHOR

In early spring of 2006 I read Geert Mak's *In Europe*. The Dutchman travelled all over Europe in 1999 and depicted the history of the twentieth century. On page 399 of the thirteenth print I read the name of Georges Kopp.

Mak describes him as a Belgian engineer who left everything to join the Spanish Republicans and fight against the fascists led by Franco. The communists arrested him, and despite the intervention of George Orwell he finally disappeared from the scene.

Why did I stop reading there? Did I feel some solidarity with a fellow countryman? Did his disappearance tickle my imagination? Or was it the dramatic history that appealed to me – you fight for a good cause and then your allies throw you in prison. Or was I intrigued that Orwell, in my opinion one of the most important writers of the twentieth century, had wanted to help him?

Georges Kopp would eventually occupy me for several years. I consulted some sources at random and fell from one surprise to another: Kopp had not died in a Spanish dungeon and he was no Belgian citizen. I decided to dig deeper, and I came across files of the British espionage service MI5, the Belgian alien registration service and the French Foreign Legion. The search led me to the families of my protagonist. I travelled to Genval near Brussels, Belgium and met his eldest daughter Anne-Marie. Quentin, his youngest son, received me in Pilsley near Chesterfield, UK. And Michel, his eldest son, and Christophe, his grandson, gave me some missing pieces of information.

And how could I know what the Spanish Civil War had meant without visiting Barcelona? On the lively Plaça de Catalunya, surrounded by stately buildings, it wasn't difficult to imagine how the red banners had waved in the city at the beginning of the war. But the abolition of the classes did not unite the Left, and the city fell into the hands of the fascist troops. Some years later I would visit Huesca, Barbastro, Leciñena and Alcubierre to walk in the trenches in which Kopp and Orwell had fought.

It was originally my intention to process the material into a novel, but I never found the right tone. Working with primary sources had given me so much satisfaction that writing a novel would not seem to do justice to the subject. Eventually I decided to write a historical biography of my protagonist.

Georges Kopp was a fascinating figure, but it was his friendship with George Orwell that won him his place in history. No biographer of Orwell fails to mention Kopp. Orwell is still an icon in the English-speaking world, and if you read his work for a second time, you realize why. And I refer not only to the classics, but also to the surprisingly timeless *Homage to Catalonia*, an eyewitness report on the Spanish Civil War. Kopp is mentioned several times throughout the text, and there is no doubt that Orwell's view on the world was influenced by him. In my opinion *1984*'s O'Brien and the infamous Room 101, for example, cannot be seen separately from Kopp.

In all honesty I can say that Kopp is someone who won his spurs without Orwell. The combination of his idealism, fearlessness and intelligence drove him into situations which he did not always control. It was sometimes difficult for him to separate lies from fantasy, and he was full of contradictions, but this made my historical research all the more rewarding.

Georges Kopp is a figure that challenges you to enter into his labyrinth.

Chapter 1

THE BEGINNINGS OF A
TURBULENT LIFE

Georges Kopp was born in St Petersburg on 23rd June 1902. Both
his parents came from Russia: his father, Alexander, was from Rostov-
on-Don, and his mother, Guitalia Neimann, was from Odessa.[1] Their
names, according to surviving relatives, indicate that their ancestors were
descendants of German Jews who in the eighteenth and nineteenth
century had travelled en masse to Russia, where they had put unprocessed
farming land into use at the instigation of Catherine the Great.[2]
According to the same relatives, Alexander Kopp was a socialist doctor
who had opposed the Tsar, and this was the reason he had had to flee.[3]

In 1909 the family arrived in Schaerbeek, Belgium.[4] Guitalia
Neimann changed her name to Henriette upon arrival in

Henriette Neimann with her grandchildren, from left to right:
Michel, Jean and Pierre[5]

Brussels. The Belgian immigration police, who checked all data with the Russian police, could not find any Alexander Kopp in St Petersburg. If father Alexander was a physician, he never practised his profession in Belgium – he earned his living as a sales representative.

In 1915 the Kopp family immigrated to Lausanne.[6] They later reappeared in the municipal registers of Schaerbeek on 9th April 1920. Georges Kopp studied civil engineering at the Université Libre de Bruxelles (ULB), completing his first and second year. But when his father died on Christmas Day 1921 he had to cancel his studies. According to his daughter Anne-Marie he took over his father's debt as a true Russian, which put him in a difficult position before he had even begun his professional life. To cope with his debt, he worked as an engineer. Finding a job was no trouble for him – even an unfinished university degree was of great value – and from 1923 to 1931 he worked for the Société Chaurobel, a metallurgic plant in Brussels.[7]

On 12th May 1925 the young Kopp plunged into a marriage with Germaine Warnotte, his childhood sweetheart, who had lived opposite him in the same street in Schaerbeek.[8] Anne-Marie shared an anecdote concerning their first meeting. Little Georges had contracted the infectious scarlet fever and was exiled to his room. Out of boredom he wrote 'I'm sick' in Russian on the steamy window of his room. To his surprise someone replied in the house across the street, also writing 'I'm sick' in Russian. George ran to his parents stating that the neighbours were Russians. In reality it was Germaine's father, Daniel Warnotte – a polyglot, who happened to be in the room of the sick Germaine – who had written the words.[9] The marriage certificate states that Kopp was Roman Catholic. According to Anne-Marie, he had converted in order to marry Germaine.

From 1931 to 1933 Kopp was working in a power plant in Langerbrugge near Ghent. In no time he had acquired some elementary Flemish, a language he added to Russian, English and French – an illustration of the skill with which he would blend into new surroundings. Still, when the economic crisis struck he had to look for another job. The family moved to Uccle and came to live in Verhulststraat 60. In 1934 he became a freelance consultant, but the one-man business didn't prosper; as a consequence Georges and Germaine experienced financial difficulties.

If you look with twenty-first-century eyes towards the circumstances in which the couple lived it is easy to see that separation was inevitable. They had five children in six years, they shared the house with Kopp's temperamental mother and financial problems were never far away.[10] Germaine could live with that, but she couldn't endure the amorous escapades of her husband and asked for a divorce – unusual at the time, especially when the initiative came from a woman. To cut a long story short: adultery was clearly proven in court, and on 9th August 1935 they officially divorced. Kopp moved in once again with his mother and found work in a steelworks in Trazegnies. Henriette Neimann could certainly not support her son financially, since she was technically a Russian refugee and lived on an allowance of only 400 Belgian francs a month.

Kopp was granted visiting rights and Anne-Marie has fond memories of those times. Germaine and the children stayed with her father. Towards the end of the weekend Georges would sometimes arrive there with his car packed with kids. The neighbours always looked bewildered, watching him while he playfully pulled the kids through his rear car window so that he didn't have to open the doors.

According to his eldest daughter, he complied with his maintenance obligation irregularly. The will was certainly there, but not always the money, as illustrated by a document from his Immigration Department file. The letter from F. Salmain & Sons in Brussels (suppliers of governments, schools, industrial buildings) springs to mind because of the beautiful letterhead, designed in the business style of the time. On 20th November 1939 Salmain wrote to the security services, because in 1934 the firm had received from Kopp an unsecured bill of exchange of 11,000 Belgian francs. The manager wondered whether Kopp had stayed in Belgium and if it would be worthwhile to present the bill for payment after all.[11] That Salmain saw the need to appeal to the security services speaks for itself – 11,000 Belgian francs was a serious amount, the equivalent of over 8,000 euros.[12] This confirms Kopp's precarious financial situation. Later, his MI5 file mentions his financial problems as one of the reasons for his divorce.

GRANDE BRASSERIE HOTEL SALA

CHAUFFAGE CENTRAL · EAU COURANTE · SALLES DE BAINS

SERVICE A PRIX FIXE ET A LA CARTE
ON PREND DES PENSIONNAIRES
ON SERT A TOUTE HEURE
REPAS SUR COMMANDE
SPÉCIALITÉ DE RÉVEILLONS
CONSOMMATIONS DE MARQUE

M. SALA, Propriétaire

6, Passage des Variétés - PERPIGNAN - Tél. 12-29

DANCING

CHAMBRES CONFORTABLES
SALLE POUR FÊTES ET BANQUETS

Le 19 octobre 1936

Mes chers petits enfants chéris,

Je viens d'apprendre, à mon véritable désespoir, qu'une lettre que j'ai écrite le 6 à Paris n'a probablement pas été postée par la personne à qui je l'avais confiée et que vous ne savez, par conséquent, rien de moi depuis votre dernière [...]

Au risque de vous redire ce que j'ai déjà écrit le 6, je vais vous expliquer ce qui s'est passé.

Nous allons rester quelque temps sans nous voir car j'ai souscrit au début de mois un engagement volontaire dans les milices gouvernementales espagnoles.

Il faut que je vous explique une décision que j'ai prise après mûre réflexion et dont je désire que vous puissiez comprendre les motifs et, au besoin, les relire quand vous serez plus grands.

Depuis quelques années, il est par le monde, un courant d'idées qu'on appelle fascistes et qui vise à instituer dans chaque pays un régime de dictature, c'est à dire un [...] où toute liberté est supprimée au profit de quelques chefs. Le mouvement

After an argument with his mother in July 1936 Kopp did not return to live with her. In fact, he seemed to have disappeared from the globe. On 19th October 1936 he resurfaced again at the Hotel Sala in Perpignan, and wrote a long letter to his five children on the hotel letterhead.

His daughter Anne-Marie describes this personal document as follows: 'The letter of 19th October was very moving, and despite its private nature it can be read as a letter from a loving father to his very young children. Our ages at that time ranged from ten years for Michel to four and a half for Paul. He was in the Grande Brasserie Hotel Sala, 6 Passage des Variétés, Perpignan.'[13] The letter is translated from French, the language used by the Kopps in Belgium.

My dearest, dearest children,

I've just heard, to my sincere dismay, that a letter I wrote on the 6th in Paris was probably not posted by the person to whom I had entrusted it, and that because of this you know nothing of me since my last conversation with you. At the risk of saying to you again what I said on the 6th, I'll explain what happened. We will not see each other again for a while because I signed a voluntary agreement with the Spanish government militias at the beginning of the month. I want to explain to you this decision I have taken after careful consideration, and from this I hope that you can understand my motives, and if necessary, reread when you are grown-up.

For several months there has been in the world a school of thought that one calls fascist, and which aims to install a dictatorship in each country, i.e., a regime where all freedom is suppressed for the profit of its leaders. This movement was first successful in Italy and then Germany and Portugal, and now there is a very hard battle in Spain between the militias of the government and fascist forces.

To avoid the success of the latter, who in their wake – I know this from very good sources – will bring a civil war to Belgium, all men of good will have to give their help and support to the Republican government in Madrid.

So I decided to put myself at the service of the government, and I waited for almost two weeks in Paris to continue (where I wrote as soon as I arrived); for several hours now I've been in Perpignan, very close to the Spanish border, which I am about to cross. Once I know my address there, I will send it to you.

My dear and beloved children, my heart shrinks at the idea of leaving you and having to go so far from you. I comfort myself thinking of my good and brave children, that we love each other and that you needn't be ashamed of your father.

Little children, be as kind and thoughtful as possible to your mummy during my absence. This is my formal wish and I hope that whenever you think of me, you will remember my wish and will manage to be a source of joy and happiness for the person I haven't been able to make happy, which still brings me to a bitter mood.

I wish that my three boys Michael, Pierre and Jean will take her under their special protection…

The letter betrays a man who had lost himself after a tumultuous separation and sought rehabilitation by fighting for a noble cause. The farewell phrases show that he fully realized that death lurked around the corner. Perhaps he was looking for a heroic end.

That Kopp chose to fight for the Republicans against the fascists during the Spanish conflict fits into the family tradition: his father, Dr Alexander Kopp, may well have had a role in the opposition to the Tsar, and Georges's enrolment at the Université Libre de Bruxelles was at that time also a statement – 'Libre' stood unambiguously for 'liberal' (i.e., not Catholic).

Later he would claim during an MI5 interrogation that 'at the time he had no more sympathy for the Republican army than for the Monarchists, but it was easier for him to join the former by applying at the Spanish Embassy in BELGIUM'.[14] I'm quite confident that Kopp said this because he did not want to be associated too strongly with communism. This would have excluded him from collaboration with MI5.[15]

All in all we can safely conclude that Kopp was not a typical 'red rascal'. His mother later stated to the foreign state police that her son had never been politically active, and indeed we don't find his name reflected in what is chronicled on the political social life of the time.

Regardless of his choice of this or that party, it is likely that someone like Kopp, with a divorce behind him and unbridled fascism lurking, stepped cheerily into the Spanish civil conflict. His daughter Anne-Marie called him 'a Russian soul', reflecting the nostalgia and tragedy in the stories of Tolstoy, Dostoevsky and Pushkin.

A scribbled note to his ex-wife that was with the letter to his children is self-explanatory: 'In the letter to the children you have been able to read about the political reasons that make me leave, but I didn't need to explain to them why that kind of reason was

Germaine Warnotte, Kopp's first wife

A young father with Michel, his oldest son

able to touch me and has made me act right now.' He ends the note with a request to have his children educated in a Christian way. A paradoxical request, because not much later he joined the POUM: an organization which, to put it mildly, was not fond of religion.

Before our protagonist has even begun his quest as a soldier in the Spanish Civil War, we can discern the root causes of his ultimate tragic downfall in 1951. Kopp combined a lethal cocktail of contradictory elements: he was brave and inventive; he was a fabulist, a seducer, a polyglot; and he was full of fearless enterprise, the patriarch of a family he abandoned for the greater project. His ability to reinvent himself would become his trademark. You have a feeling that those he hurt, such as his ex-wife and his children, forgave him because, despite everything, he was authentic and passionate.[16]

On 21st October 1937, he was deleted from the municipal register of Schaerbeek.

Chapter 2

'A COMIC OPERA WITH AN OCCASIONAL DEATH'

Shortly after sending his letters Kopp crossed the border in order to register with the Partido Obrero de Unificación Marxista (POUM), an organization of especially idealistic Marxists led by Andrés Nin, who had at one time lived in Russia. The POUM had the reputation of being Trotskyite, although Nin had distanced himself from Trotsky in 1934. They had more in common with the leftist opposition in the Soviet Union.[1] They contrasted with, among others, the pragmatic communists of the Partido Socialista Unificado de Cataluña (PSUC), which received support from Stalin. Kopp probably did not choose the POUM for ideological reasons, but rather because it was known to be an easy militia to get into.

If we are to understand Kopp's odyssey, we must return to the beginnings of the Spanish Civil War: in 1931 the left-wing government proclaimed the country a republic after King Alfonso XIII had fled the country. The successive leftist governments did not insist on centralized rule and allowed a certain degree of autonomy for Catalonia. They failed to restore order in the country, and on 18th July 1936 the army, led by Franco, moved to overthrow the republic. Spain became torn between a Left/Republican and extreme Right/fascist side. Spaniards mistreated, tortured and killed Spaniards. Wife or husband, child or adult, young or old, priest or nun, it did not matter: 'We became familiar with all the dirty, laughable nature of wasted flesh. We knew them, just slain, for it drew a veil over their eyes, their faces pale, reserved and noble; we knew them when they were yellow and green and swollen.'[2]

Albert Helman recounts a remarkable story that illustrates the tensions, which seem incomprehensible nowadays. A priest, be it a conservative one, was shot by the Republicans for the simple fact that he was a priest: 'The priest was condemned to death, and both the militias and the civilians of Caspe treated this as totally natural. No one had expected anything else, and the only thing which interested people was the question of who would take part in the firing squad. [...] The discussion took so much time that the execution was postponed until dawn of the next morning.'[3] They burnt all the priest's possessions, including a valuable eighteenth-century manuscript.

The Right supported the absolute leader Franco. The Left at first reacted furiously and overwhelmingly, including the women: 'The militia girls were really worth remembering, as living symbols of a whole generation of women who liberated themselves from the shackles of centuries, of a triple burden of exploitation – religiously, economically and sexually. Bullets in their cartridge belts would be directed against those who defended these traditions.'[4] But beautiful songs do not last long; the Left was shattered into several factions, from traditional socialists to anarchists and communists.

The conflict caused quite a stir; 35,000 volunteers (including Kopp, Orwell and Andre Malraux) from over ten different countries helped the Republican amalgamation to defend itself against fascism. War correspondent Martha Gellhorn said afterwards, 'We knew, we just knew, that Spain was the place to stop Fascism. This was it. It was one of those moments when there was no doubt.'[5] Pablo Neruda and Ernest Hemingway also published commentaries on the conflict. The stories of Hemingway breathe the same atmosphere as Orwell's *Homage to Catalonia* – The camaraderie that grows in pubs and the nonchalance of pub brawls turn during wartime into the machinations of spies and into death.

Hemingway followed the civil war as a reporter and helped, among others, the Dutch filmmaker Joris Ivens by narrating the documentary *The Spanish Earth*. Describing an ill-fated offensive of the International Brigade, he says,

But the oddest thing about that day was how marvelously the pictures we took of the tanks came out. On the screen they advanced over the hill irresistibly, mounting the crests like great ships, to crawl clanking on toward the illusion of victory we screened.

The nearest any man was to victory that day was probably the Frenchman who came, with his head held high, walking out of the battle. But his victory only lasted until he had walked halfway down the ridge. We saw him lying stretched out there on the slope of the ridge, still wearing his blanket.[6]

The internal division of the Left, its international isolation and the interference of Hitler's troops were the main factors which led to the defeat of the Republicans in 1939, but certainly not the only ones. The inability of the leftist Republican government to unite itself will be dealt with later, but it was not their only vice. Their military leaders, helped by Soviet consultants, also failed strategically because of an obsolete tactical method consisting of offensives straight out of training manuals from World War I. They almost always attacked to draw pressure away from endangered sectors or for propaganda purposes. They failed to follow through after these surprise attacks and Nationalist troops always managed to reorganize.

The fact is that the Republicans were in urgent need of weapons and these were mainly delivered by Stalin. Great Britain and France had opted for a non-intervention policy, and they could not have made a difference in any case, as their weapons were obsolete. The only country which could have helped them was the United States, but it decided not to intervene because of the powerful Catholic lobby that supported the Nationalists.

The Germans and the Italians on the other hand actively supported Franco. 'To say that they won the war for Franco entirely would be going too far. The [German] Condor Legion above all accelerated the conquest of the north [...]. But the truly devastating effectiveness of the Condor Legion came in countering the major Republican offensives of 1937 and 1938, battles which were to break the back of the Republican armed forces.'[7]

All these factors led to the defeat of the officially elected Republican government. On 1st April 1939 Franco officially declared the end of the Spanish Civil War, which essentially meant a victory of Right ideology over Left.

Franco installed a repressive regime that continued until his death in 1975. Even now, seventy-seven years after the beginning of the civil war, the country has not yet fully come to terms with its history. On 31st October 2007 the Spanish parliament adopted the Historic Memory Law, which recognizes the victims on both sides and could lead to reconciliation between the old Left and Right forces.

In October 1936, the revolution in Catalonia and Aragon had already passed its peak. After Franco's military coup of 18th July was repulsed, many different political parties and unions in Barcelona formed separate militias. Together with some loyal remnants of the regular army – the rest deserted to Franco – they had managed to fix Franco's troops on a front line that ran from Huesca in the north to the south of Teruel. That line remained there for eighteen months.

In that month Kopp signed up to the 29th Division, previously known as the Lenin Division, of the POUM. He told them he was a Belgian citizen and had served as a reservist officer in the army. In his own words he had made and shipped illegal ammunition to the Republicans in Spain despite an arms embargo. Then he fled from Belgium and abandoned his family. Finally he claimed that his wife had died while giving birth to their fourth child. We can say with certitude that, despite the fact that he claimed to be a Belgian all his life, Kopp had never had Belgian nationality, let alone been in the Belgian army, nor had he ever made any ammunition.[8] Not to mention that his wife was still alive and he had five children. Why he fabricated such blatant lies we can only guess. Did he not want to serve as an ordinary member of the militia? Did he want to avoid a boring training period and immediately aim for a higher rank? Or was it his intention to cover his tracks and avoid troubling questions about his divorce or his precarious financial situation?

Kopp obviously had the advantage that the POUM could not retrieve his data in Belgium. Officially, Belgium, and thus the Belgian army, was neutral. Unofficially there was more sympathy among Belgian military personnel for the Nationalists of Franco. From then until now, total confusion reigns over who Kopp really was. Take the trouble to Google him and you can turn theory into practice – the search for the real figure is a textbook case for a course in historical criticism. Kopp is turned to 'Kapp', for example, by the historian David Mitchell. Half of the sources still see him as a Belgian soldier. Sometimes he is widower. For some he sympathizes with the fascists, while more recently Rob Stradling suspects him of being a Stalinist double spy.[9] Noam Chomsky, a renowned political analyst and linguist, calls Kopp a Trotskyite general. Painful, because he uses the Kopp case precisely to show that the Stalinists twisted history, while he himself is, be it unintentionally, doing the same.

In any case Kopp knew how to obscure his lack of experience masterfully. Anne-Marie Kopp calls him brilliant, versatile and exuberant. For example, he spoke six to eight languages including Russian, Spanish, French and English.[10] What he lacked in experience he will undoubtedly have been able to compensate for in verbal ability and intelligence. If there was a militia in which he could get away with it, then it would have been the POUM, where idealism and good will ruled. Their efficiency, however, was lacking. They barely had any rifles, so they just learnt to parade, and serious training would only ever come *mañana* (i.e., never).[11] The other Republican groups didn't feel much like giving weapons to militia members of the extreme Left.

Just as Kopp had volunteered, the Generalidad (the Catalan government) tried, while collaborating with the central Republican government in Madrid but insisting on its independence, to forge an efficient army of the heterogeneous, predominantly left-wing militias. As of 6th December 1936, these militias joined the Catalan army and a military hierarchy was reintroduced. Before this, everyone received the same pay, and in the POUM especially, officers had no visible signs of their rank and saluting was not practised. But that was the past. Kopp came in at this turning point and swiftly took his place in the new hierarchy.

From the end of October until the end of December 1936, there are two sources which describe Kopp's activities: the magazine *L'Espagne Nouvelle* and the *Independent News*. They both probably used Kopp as their sole witness.[12] He states that he was sent to the Aragon front; first to Casetas near Zaragoza on 9th October, and then to Huesca on 21st October. This seems strange as the letter to his children written from Perpignan is dated 19th October 1936. He claims to have fought in November near the Manicomio (a former lunatic asylum on the outskirts of Huesca, where POUM shock troops launched an unsuccessful attack to recapture it), and in Vedado-Zuero (between Huesca and Zaragoza) on 5th December.[13]

By the end of December 1936 Kopp had already made it to commander of his *centuria*, leading a company of between eighty and a hundred men in the Miguel Pedrola Column.[14] This is when he met George Orwell, who had arrived in Barcelona on the 26th of December. Kopp was checking the list of new recruits for the front when he saw 'grocer' next to the name of Orwell. He found that occupation did not fit the strange, intellectual-looking beanpole before him. Yet it is true in part because Orwell and his wife Eileen O'Shaughnessy were living in Britain in 'The Stores', a house which had a small grocer's shop. Kopp would never have guessed that that particular broomstick would assure him of a place in history.

Orwell, like Kopp, ended up with the POUM rather by coincidence – in his case, because he had papers for the British Independent Labour Party.[15] The writer had just finished training in the Lenin Barracks in Barcelona. He had absolutely no idea then that there was such a difference between the Left parties. He enjoyed Barcelona, steeped as it was in the revolution. Despite the many red flags, the city looked grey and there was a food shortage. Still, most of the 'comrades' seemed satisfied because there was no unemployment. Beggars and rich bourgeoisie seemed to have gone up in smoke and revolutionary music was blaring through the streets. Hairdressers and plumbers were called on to free themselves from capitalism. Prostitutes threw off the yoke of oppression. But in reality, the rich merely tolerated classless society, waiting until a new leader would stand up to reinstall the old regime: women couldn't wear fancy hats anymore because that was a sign of the higher classes. But then one underestimates the resourcefulness of wo(man)… they started having nice perms which the poorer classes couldn't afford.[16] Orwell realized that innocence would eventually be defiled and that the counter-revolution was already lurking, but it was a thought he pushed away for the time being.

It is difficult to understand the military structure of the POUM and the Spanish Republican Army. In his *Homage to Catalonia* Orwell tries to compare the ranks to the British hierarchy, but this is not appropriate. Later in his story, for example, Orwell calls Kopp a major; no such data, however, can be found in any military archives.[17] The highest rank Kopp ever reached was that of captain (this will be explained later). The Spaniard Josep Rovira was the commander-in-chief of the

29th Division, which was active on the Aragon front and consisted of 3000 men. The battalion Kopp and Orwell served in had 500 to 750 militants with Gregorio Jorge, Kopp's good friend, as its commander. Orwell was a member of the ILP contingent, a group of mainly British and Irish volunteers that were incorporated into the 29th Division. The rest of the 29th consisted of Spaniards and people of other nationalities such as Americans and Germans. Orwell became a corporal and a political commissar (a delegate for the War Committee of the POUM), thanks to his ability to speak some Catalan.[18]

As stated before, there aren't that many sources which describe Kopp's activities during the Spanish Civil War, so we have to rely mainly on Orwell's *Homage*, and he is only mentioned in parts of the account. We assume that most of his activities coincide with Orwell's, although we know that Kopp travelled to Barcelona more often since he was a company commander. So let us return to Orwell's arrival in Barcelona.

Orwell describes how the Lenin Barracks, which were once proud stone buildings for the cavalry, had turned into a state of filth. Every building was littered with smashed furniture and decaying food – one of the by-products of revolution, he adds ironically. Two days after his arrival Orwell was made a sergeant and was drilling the young recruits. The Spanish tried to get him drunk on their red wine, but failed as he had become accustomed to drinking cheap red wine while living in Paris.

After one week Orwell left with his colourful troop. In Barcelona people had a kind of motto to indicate the POUM militia: 'Piem, Pam, Poum, fire away!'[19] First they paraded with torches past cheering crowds along the Ramblas, and then were put on a train to Aragon. There the front line was closest to Barcelona. It cut Aragon into two parts: a Republican part, northeast of Zaragoza, and a Nationalist part, west of that line. Most of the time, the front line followed the Sierra de Alcubierre. From July 1936 onwards the main military efforts of the POUM militia were on the Aragon front. The goal, together with various other leftist parties, was to recapture Zaragoza. The POUM militia advanced as far as Leciñena, but there the offensive stalled. In September they even lost it again. You can still find pencil-drawn images of Nationalist soldiers on the walls of the barracks in Leciñena, which overlooks the Sierra de Alcubierre. It now serves as a hotel.

Orwell arrived by train to Barbastro, still a long way from the front. Then the company was sent by lorry to Siétamo and further to Alcubierre. The driver lost his way in the fog and it was late at night before they reached Alcubierre, situated 460 metres above sea level and terribly cold, since it was January. They had to wade through the mud before they finally found a mule stable and could sleep on layers of chaff. The next morning he discovered that the chaff was mixed with bread crusts, torn newspaper, dead rats and other debris. In Alcubierre he was confronted with the smell of decaying food and excrement, especially in the church because it had been used as a latrine. The stench and the cold would never leave him during his stay on the front. After two days in the small town, nothing had happened. The only excitement was an inspection of the row of bullet holes in the wall of the town hall where several fascists had been shot. The locals had been brought over from Lanaja so that there would not be too much trouble during the execution.[20] There was also a POUM hospital and headquarters, both situated along the main road.

The POUM headquarters in Alcubierre. Georges Kopp must have been here many times[21]

The POUM hospital in Alcubierre. Orwell must have seen it,
but does not mention it[22]

On the third morning the rifles arrived, be it of very bad quality,
and they finally left for the front. A group of about eighty men
marched, or rather shuffled, forward in a chaotic row. Half of them
were sixteen or younger and had no combat experience. Many wore
rags. Orwell wore his rusty Mauser of 1896. 'The best rifle had
been given to a half-witted little beast of fifteen, known to everyone
as the *maricón* (Nancy-boy).'[23] Some dogs accompanied them as
mascots: one of the poor animals had had 'POUM' branded into its
fur. The irregular crackle of machine guns sounded in the distance.
He thought in fear of the cold mud in the trenches in which he would
soon end up. He still tasted a hastily eaten can of beans. And then
ahead of that ragged bunch rode Kopp the 'commandante', seated
on a black horse, a red flag waving next to him.

This image gave Orwell confidence. It did not matter that the
horse was captured from the fascists. If Orwell had known that
Kopp knew less of combat techniques than he did – Orwell had
been a policeman in Burma – he would have judged his commander
differently. Not that Orwell had no opportunity to observe Kopp; the
front line barely moved an inch, so they had plenty of time to kill and
grew quite fond of one another. In theory the Republicans wanted
to capture Zaragoza; in reality both Republicans and fascists licked

their wounds and had no other goal but to consolidate their positions. Kopp outlined this period of boredom and intermittent skirmishes in his inimitable way as 'a comic opera with an occasional death'.[24] It is quite normal for an international mix of mostly idealistic men looking for adventure, given plenty of spare time, to forge a close relationship. The next scene on the front of Aragon illustrates the, at times, boyish friendship between Orwell and Kopp: 'Close in front a bugle-call rings out from the Fascist lines. Kopp catches my eye and, with a schoolboy gesture, thumbs his nose at the sound'.[25] It is reminiscent of two scouts somewhere, lying behind a bush during a game. Because they cannot talk, they pull faces to say 'Ugh, the enemy'.

It remains surprising that Orwell, a merciless observer, believed most of the story that Kopp had invented until years after the Spanish Civil War. Orwell thought, certainly in the beginning, that Kopp had sacrificed his family and career to fight against the Spanish fascists. To make matters worse he even risked a prison sentence once he returned home, because he had left the Belgian territory without permission as a reserve officer. On top of it all he was supposed to have made ammunition illegally for the leftist Spanish government. It turned out that Orwell and his friends did not buy the whole story, although they never questioned him.[26]

Unlike the other officers of the POUM, Kopp was keen on wearing epaulets – he believed in the concept of hierarchy and authority.[27] Maybe he was also keen on the uniform because he could be the officer that he never had been in the Belgian army. Fortunately he had more to offer than parading in a uniform. His dedication and courage run like a thread through all his personal stories of the civil war.

Bob Edwards, for example, commander of the ILP contingent in Spain and after World War II a Labour member of parliament, dedicated a long article to Georges Kopp on page two of the *New Leader* of 13th August 1937, titled 'Soldier of Socialism'.[28] The text is a mixture of lies and truth. Edwards calls him 'Goth', but above the article he explains that Goth is in fact Kopp. The author explains that the incidents on the Aragon front are true, but fused into one sequence. He also changes the place names – perhaps for safety reasons – but they can easily be decoded for someone who has visited the area: 'Barasster' is Barbastro, the 'village' is Alcubierre and 'Monte Ivore' is Monte Irazo. Probably for the same reason the name POUM cannot be found. It is a valuable article because, just like Orwell, Edwards depicts the appearance and the personality of Kopp in detail. Both descriptions match and must therefore be conclusive. Still, we have to remain critical because Edwards does not question the numerous lies that Kopp confides to him:

Suddenly out of the darkness loomed three figures in the picturesque uniform of the Spanish Militia. 'Welcome to the Front,' came a voice in cultured English with just a slight accent. [...] By the flickering light of the match I saw his face, a commanding, almost handsome face with a strong dimpled chin, laughing lips and blue, mischievous eyes surmounted by a broad, smooth brow. My first impression was that it was the face of a German or, maybe, a Dutchman. He gave me a quick, mischievous, yet searching look. A quiet courage seemed to emanate from him. [...] It was three weeks later when I heard his story. We were inspecting the lines – nine fortified mountain crests in the foothills of Aragon. Our patrols had reported great activity behind the enemy lines. The head lights of convoys had been seen by our night guards far back in the distance; and in the distance too, were those church bells I heard? My companion, Goth, confirmed my thoughts with a shrug. 'Yes, Fascist church bells – that leaves little doubt about the expected attack. [...] Oh, yes didn't you know – all Fascist attacks are previously "blessed" by church service.' He added bitterly: 'Invoking the assistance of the Gentle Nazarene, even when it involves the slaughter of the aged, the sick and the babies. Who was it of your English who said: 'Ye hypocrites! Are these your pranks? To murder men and give God thanks?'[29] [...] Presently, we came to rest for a while to regain our wind for the next climb to our most important position – a mountain crest, Mount Ivore, which dominated the Huesca-Saragossa road.

My companion rolled a cigarette with expert fingers. He looked not at me but beyond me. 'Let me see – it's Thursday today?' I nod a confirmation. Glancing at his watch he continued slowly: 'At about this time I might be having pork chops with apple sauce and baked potatoes with a pint of English brew and a good cigar. That, just now, would be perfect. I'd give a good deal for just one day in Brussels. [...] My home is in Brussels.'

Then Kopp's usual 'cover' story is repeated: the manufacturing of ammunition, being a reservist officer in the Belgian army, the death of his wife in childbirth and his flight from Belgium. That he is not the most modest type of character is illustrated by the following:

'I was chief engineer,' he continued, 'employed by one of the largest engineering firms in Belgium. It was quite a good post. Let me see, my salary in English would be about £1,000 a year. Would you call that a good job in England?'

'We certainly would!' I replied. 'You must have been pretty efficient to demand that salary.' 'Yes,' he replied. 'In terms of £.s.d. it was a very good post, but I earned every cent of it. My firm made thousands out of my inventions and ideas.'

As a soldier Kopp must have been quite impressive: 'I can well remember, even in these circumstances, marvelling at the surprising agility of George Goth in spite of his thirteen stone. He was always ahead of me, light-footed as a mountain goat, moving up that dangerous hillside with amazing rapidity.' The article ends with the perhaps obsequious but nevertheless true words: 'George Goth, I salute you! Soldier of Socialism, man without a country, citizen of the world!'

The Sierra de Alcubierre is part of Los Monegros. It is a hilly region with horseshoe-shaped formations with flat tops and steep ravines; a semi-desert with stones, stunted shrubs and heath. The front line was not one fortified long line of trenches, but a series of fortifications that were situated at the top of the hills. The Nationalists and Republicans were separated by a wasteland of some hundred metres and 'zigzagged to and fro in a pattern that would have been quite unintelligible if every position had not had a flag'.[30] Orwell's position was situated on a hill called Monte Pucero and the Nationalists' on

'La Impossible'. It was indeed hardly possible to take that hill unless you first descended into the ravine and climbed the steep hill while being heavily shelled and shot at by enemy soldiers.

Nothing happened during the three weeks Kopp and Orwell were in that position. Orwell sums up five things in order of importance which occupied the militia: 'firewood, food, tobacco, candles and the enemy'.[31] It took a militiaman some hours to collect wood on the steep hills, often in darkness. He couldn't do that without constantly falling, which was dangerous because his rifle would become jammed by the mud. He was then able to maintain a fire for about an hour. The alternative was getting dressed in several layers of clothes, and even then the damp cold would get hold of him.

There Orwell realized that the political Left was no unity: 'At Monte Pucero, when they pointed to the position on our left and said: "Those are the Socialists" (meaning the PSUC), I was puzzled and said: "Aren't we all Socialists?"'[32]

Three weeks later, Orwell and probably Kopp moved their positions to Monte Irazo, one mile to the south of Monte Pucero and more than 800 meters above sea level.[33] There they joined the newly arrived members of the ILP contingent. Bob Edwards was the commander of the British group and Kopp stayed the overall centuria commander: 'The English contingent is behaving splendidly. To illustrate the point, I want to tell you this. I thought of moving Bob's group to another strategic position for military reasons, but the Spanish comrades near them protested, saying they felt safe in their vicinity and did not want to have any other neighbours.'[34] 'Bob' is Bob Smillie, a prominent member of the contingent. We can conclude that the British and Irish militiamen were in good spirits and got along fine with their group of some twelve Spanish machine-gunners and Spanish soldiers of other militia. The Spanish knew two English expressions well: 'OK baby' and 'fuck'.[35] Still, nothing much happened. To kill time Orwell read Shakespeare and detective novels and wrote letters or comments. He was certainly not the only one: recent archaeological excavations during trench reconstructions where Orwell stayed produced masses of glass ink pots.[36]

Orwell's 'All Quiet on the Monte Irazo Front' is somehow contradicted by Bob Edwards's article of 13th August 1937.[37]

This can be explained by the fact that Edwards fused several stories into one article. Consequently events in the article needn't have happened on Monte Ivore (i.e., Monte Irazo). Still, it is worthwhile using it because Goth, alias Kopp, plays a major role:

> Suddenly our silent communion was broken by the menacing thunder of heavy gunfire in the distance, followed a few seconds later by the deafening explosions of the shells. One exploded on the opposite side of the hill in front of us. We could hear the scream of it before it landed. Immediately we were on our feet. The change in my companion was amazing. His features were tense, hard and cold. We scrambled up the hillside in the direction of Mount Ivore. [...]
>
> By the time we reached Mount Ivore all was quiet. [...] The first sight to meet us brought relief – and then came a feeling of horror. A group of a dozen or so militia men were working feverishly, clearing the entrance of what must once have been a large dug-out, working with spades, hands and rifle-butts, clearing away the debris.
>
> One man especially attracted my attention. I can see him now, pathetic, tragic, and yet so brave. A man with the stripes of a sergeant, with a fine intelligent face and the physique of a youth. Blood streaked his snow-white hair. He was swaying as he tore great rocks away with his hands that were torn and bleeding. Later I learned that his only son was one of the thirteen killed in the dug-out by a shell which dropped through the roof. [...] With a heavy heart I retraced my steps, giving a farewell salute to my recent companion, busily occupied organising the reconstruction of the ruined fortification. I know that you loved those brave Spanish lads as they loved and respected you.

On 16th February 1937, two weeks later, the 29th Division of the POUM left Monte Irazo for Huesca, where they could expect more combat experience. Nationalist and Republican troops had fought long and fiercely for the positions east of town, with heavy material and personal losses as a result. After that the Republicans encircled the town with a system of more than ninety kilometres of trenches.

View from Monte Irazo, Orwell and Kopp's second position
on Monte Pucero, their first position

Their fortified positions were as close as three to six hundred metres
from Huesca. Several times the Republicans had been on the verge of
capturing it, but to no avail.

The POUM militia had their military command post in the ruined
village of Tierz, east of Huesca.[38] One part of the 29th intended
to concentrate north of Tierz, around the road from Huesca to
Barbastro; Kopp and Orwell's unit focused on the region south of
Tierz, close to the road to Sariñena. They quartered in and around
La Granja, a farmhouse. According to Orwell its chapel, inner courts
and outbuildings lent it the appearance of a former monastery.
Unfortunately for Orwell (since he wanted action), most fighting
happened in the northern region. In the south there was a stalemate
because of the lack of heavy material to launch a serious attack.
There were skirmishes and interrupted attacks which cost lives: 'And
then waiting fifty or sixty yards from the Fascist parapet for the order
to attack. [...] Kopp and Benjamin squatting behind us with a man
who had a wireless receiving-box strapped to his shoulders.[39] [...]
And then a pip-pip-pip-noise from the wireless and the whispered

order that we were to get out of it while the going was good. We did so, but not quickly enough.'[40] Twelve members of the JCI, the youth movement of the POUM, were surprised by the dawn. Seven youngsters were shot during the day.

In La Granja they were confronted with gigantic rats, Orwell's strongest phobia (which influenced his literary career). This also had some funny side effects: one day Orwell shot an overly venturous rat, but the explosion reverberated throughout the whole front and both sides started shelling and shooting. The result was the loss of two buses used to bring up reserve troops and a cookhouse.

Just like Kopp, Orwell was almost fearless. 640 metres from their own trenches and close to a Nationalist machine gun was a potato field. Although he knew they would take shots at him, Orwell went on looking for potatoes three times a week.[41]

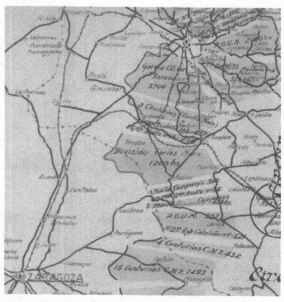

The positions of the Republicans, and more specifically of the POUM, on 29th November 1936. They stayed more or less the same during Kopp's and Orwell's active military activity. First their positions were situated near Alcubierre, later near Huesca[42]

La Granja, the farmhouse used as quarters for Orwell and Kopp's unit[43]

On 16th or 17th February Eileen O'Shaughnessy, Orwell's wife, arrived in Spain to be near her husband and to work as secretary to John McNair, head of the ILP office in Barcelona.[44] Around 13th March she managed to visit him because he was taken to a hospital in Monflorite with blood poisoning in his hand.[45] Eileen spent three days with him and brought tobacco, tea, cigars, chocolate and biscuits to supplement their rations; she even succeeded in bringing Kopp's favourite Lea & Perrins Worcester Sauce. During the last day of her stay she joined her husband at the front. Needless to say she was very popular among the men. She was quite thrilled when there was a brief exchange of fire across the lines.[46] It was Georges Kopp who drove her back to Barcelona.

On 13th April 1937 Orwell, some Spanish and several members of the ILP contingent volunteered to raid the reinforcements of the fascists near Ermita Salas in the hope of alleviating pressure on the anarchists on the other side of Huesca. It was Kopp's genius that led them to strike at night: 'Kopp addressed us, first in Spanish, then in English, and explained the attack. The Fascist line here made an L-bend and the parapet we were to attack lay on rising ground at the corner of the L.'[47]

The militia members sneaked to the enemy lines, cut the outer and inner barbed wire and threw some grenades. They managed to take some trenches for some time and cause some casualties. Orwell laconically portrays how he chased a fascist with his bayonet and failed to plunge it between the enemy's shoulders. Thanks to their surprise attack they had about half an hour to capture ammunition, a precious telescope and some grenades. The machine gun they were after in the first place had been taken by the Nationalists. To their surprise they noticed that the enemy only possessed some blankets and some damp pieces of bread. The counterattack was fierce and they were forced to withdraw hastily, Orwell to his dismay heavily wounding a fascist in the process. In the end they had to abandon the telescope. Some of them were wounded; Kopp was waiting for them and saw to it that they were brought to ambulances. He was upset:

> It appeared that all the wounded had been got in except Jorge [...].[48] Kopp was pacing up and down, very pale. Even the fat folds at the back of his neck were pale; he was paying no attention to the bullets that streamed over the low parapet and cracked close to his head. Most of us were squatting behind the parapet for cover. Kopp was muttering. 'Jorge! Coño! Jorge!' And then in English: 'If Jorge is gone it is terreeble, terreeble!' Jorge was his personal friend and one of his best officers.'

Later it transpired that Jorge had been taken to the dressing station earlier.

Here we can quote Kopp himself. On 16th April he wrote a letter to the parents of Bob Smillie describing the attack:

> *We have had some very 'hot' days and have made an advance of some thousand yards; the enemy counter-attacked but did not succeed in regaining an inch of the lost ground. In the night of the 13th we made a somewhat audacious raid on the enemy's positions on the Ermita Salas, in order to relieve pressure on the Ascaso Front [...] We have had a complete success which is due largely to courage and discipline of the English comrades who were in charge of assaulting the principal of the enemy's parapets. Among them I feel it my duty to give a particular*

mention of the splendid action of Eric Blair [George Orwell], *Bob Smillie and Paddy Donovan.*[49]

In the *New Leader* the raid was described as a heroic action, but Harry Milton, an American member of the ILP contingent, was less impressed: 'And we had only one real go at the enemy. It was the first time we went into action. It was a hellish business; the whole thing was botched up.'[50] One thing is certain: the positions of both parties did not change after the raid. Orwell, and probably Kopp too, had gradually become more and more frustrated because of the stalemate situation in Aragon, and they considered quitting the POUM and joining the International Brigades so that they could fight in Madrid, where the situation was precarious for the Republicans.[51]

Few pictures of Kopp have survived. In the most interesting photo he stands against a wall of sandbags of about one and a half metres in height. Kopp seems tall – in reality he was 1.74 metres.[52] He wears a uniform with epaulets, matching corduroy breeches and riding boots. Around his waist you can see a belt with a leather pouch and to the side a belt pouch with a revolver. He has a small pair of binoculars around his neck and on his head a kepi. He is holding his left arm behind his back. His right arm is pointing downwards and between middle finger and index finger is a cigarette. His uniform is too tight, which accentuates his tendency to corpulence.

He has big, thick lips and a large head. You could call his nose fleshy. Kopp is presumably looking towards the light, as his deeply sunken eyes are slightly squinted. In other photographs you can see his pepper-coloured hair and light eyebrows. He seems to look rather smugly into the lens, and his overall attitude betrays this. He keeps his right leg relaxed in front of his stretched left leg. Josep Pané contrasts him with his friend Gregorio Jorge, his superior officer, describing them as lookalikes of Stan Laurel and Oliver Hardy.[53]

Another photo illustrates the atmosphere at the front, and you may be surprised at the shabby clothes most of the Poumistas wore.[54] The photo shows a row of fighters aiming their weapons through the loopholes that are made in the parapet of sandbags. The shot seems to be staged. If you look to the third person to the right and you compare it to the photo above you can see the same trousers,

Orwell Archive, UCL Special Collections

Orwell Archive, UCL Special Collections

the same boots, identical belt and epaulets, the same figure. Only the soldier's cap seems to not match. If it is Kopp, his backside is more flattering and one can understand better why he is referred to as 'athletic' on the Fundación Andreu Nin website.[55]

Chapter 3

ON HEROISM AND BANALITY

In the spring of 1937, tensions between the several groups of Republicans grew. The power of the Partido Socialista Unificado de Cataluña, a regional party dominated by the communists, became more prominent in the local government of Catalonia. The PSUC owed that power to the substantial material support which Stalin granted the Spanish Republic in the form of weapons, among other items. The party, together with the socialists and regionalists, wanted a pragmatic policy; their motto was 'Victory first, revolution later'. The anarchists and Poumistas wanted to move the other way round.[1] They organized people's courts, which sometimes functioned arbitrarily, and collectivized possessions of the church and the bourgeoisie. Stalin was afraid – a paradox for a communist – that the state of confusion in Barcelona would cause a complete Spanish revolution. He was concerned that he would provoke Hitler's Germany and squander a possible future collaboration with the Allied forces if he consented to a total revolution.

Behind the screens the communists began to infiltrate and manipulate the conglomerate of Republican parties. They posted Stalinists in key positions, and if the military hierarchy expressed any doubts, they threatened that Stalin would withdraw his military support. In the meantime the NKVD, the Russian secret police, took command over the SIM, the intelligence service of the Republican army.[2] Dissidents were arrested and some of them even executed for treachery. Communists and anarchists waged a propaganda war and blamed each other for the malaise.

On 3rd May 1937, three lorries loaded with pro-government Assault Guards stopped in front of the telephone exchange on the Plaça de Catalunya, in the heart of Barcelona.[3] The anarchists were occupying the building because it enabled them to monitor politicians. The Assault Guards easily disarmed the sentinels, but the

The telephone exchange on the Plaça de Catalunya[4]

anarchists in the telephone exchange itself started spraying bullets from a machine gun. Labourers then came out of nowhere, circled the pro-government troops and built barricades. The skirmishes spread to the Ramblas, the lifeblood of the town, and led to a general strike and to street fighting that lasted for six days.

Around that time Orwell and his commander Kopp were on leave, and so happened to be around when the events of that May began. Their leave had started on 25th April and both of them were regaining their strength: having baths, enjoying a good meal and catching up on sleep before they would return to the front.[5] On the afternoon of 3rd May, Orwell was strolling on the Ramblas towards the Hotel Continental on the corner of Plaça de Catalunya to join Eileen. The telephone exchange was situated on the other side of the square. Although he had felt the tension

Hotel Falcon, lodgings of the POUM[6]

hanging around in the city, he had no idea that he was about to land in the middle of a street fight. All of a sudden the assault guards opened fire on the anarchists from their position in the octagonal tower of the church of Santa Maria del Pi, situated in the Carrer del Cardenal Casañas, a side street of the Ramblas. He couldn't move on, so he headed to the Hotel Falcon down the other end of the Ramblas, which was used by POUM militiamen on leave. No one knew what to do and gradually most of the ILP contingent gathered there to find out what was going on. The head of the ILP office, John McNair, appeared that night with supplies of cigarettes and some news.

The following day Orwell took some tobacco, a rifle and ammunition, defied the snipers and managed to work his way up the Ramblas to the Continental, where he found Eileen in the company of Kopp. Close to the Continental were the offices of the POUM. Next door was the Café Moka, where twenty to thirty Assault Guards had barricaded themselves the day before. Some German POUM shock troopers were bowling grenades down the pavement at the café to protect Harry Milton, an American member of the ILP contingent,

Café Moka on the Ramblas, occupied by the Assault Guards in May 1937[9]

The Poliorama and its observatory facing Café Moka and the
headquarters of the POUM[10]

who had to fling himself behind the kiosk for cover.[7] Although Orwell
and Kopp were instinctively supportive of the anarchists, they tried to
prevent violence. Kopp did not hesitate to intervene. He stepped onto
the street and pulled back a German who was about to draw the pin
from a grenade, shouting in several languages that they had to avoid
bloodshed. He strolled up to the café with a studied casualness, took
off his pistol and laid it down on the ground. Two Spanish militia
members did the same. Orwell later wrote, 'It was a thing I would not
have done for twenty pounds.'[8] He reached a local truce and promised
to get rid of two unexploded grenades on the pavement which were
a danger to everyone. A German fired at one and it exploded. Orwell
had a go at the other one but missed. It was the only shot he would
fire during the events of May 1937.

Kopp commanded the POUM building to be defended against
an attack, but otherwise there was to be no shooting. He sent Orwell
across the road to install himself in the observatory on the roof of
the Poliorama, a building in a vaguely art deco style. For the next
three or four days Orwell and some members of the contingent sat

there guarding the offices of the POUM. Some others decided to stay neutral because it was 'only a dust-up between the Anarchists and the police – it doesn't mean anything'.[11] In the meantime Kopp had become friendly with the Assault Guards by trading a rifle they had lost for fifteen bottles of beer. Orwell read Penguin books, ate the goat cheese which he had bought on his way to the Continental and philosophized: 'I used to sit on the roof marvelling at the folly of it all. From the little windows in the observatory you could see for miles around. […] And the whole huge town of a million people was locked in a sort of violent inertia, a nightmare of noise without movement.'[12] On 5th May Kopp sent for Orwell, 'and with a grave face, told me that according to information he had just received, the Government was about to outlaw the POUM and declare a state of war upon it'.[13]

The situation abruptly changed on 7th May when 5000 Assault Guards were brought from Valencia. The anarchists and Poumistas abandoned the telephone exchange, the Poliorama and the Ramblas. Orwell and a red-haired Spanish boy smuggled six rifles out of the building: 'Each of us partially undressed and slung a rifle over the left shoulder, the butt under the armpit, the barrel down the trouser-leg. […] Once in the street, we found that the only way to move was with extreme slowness, so slowly that you did not have to move your knees. Outside the picture-house I saw a group of people staring at me with great interest as I crept along at tortoise-speed.'[14] Thus ended this incident in a mixture of idealism, courage and amateurism, which is characteristic of the many foreigners who ended up in the Spanish Civil War.

On 8th May it was all over. 500 people had lost their lives, mostly anarchists who had a habit of charging recklessly against machine guns. Orwell was disillusioned: 'It was one of the most unbearable periods of my life. I think few experiences could be more sickening, more disillusioning or, finally, more nerve-racking than those evil days of street warfare.' The communists had a pretext to openly denounce the POUM as a fascist organization because they were hindering the Republican cause. Inside the Hotel Continental the atmosphere had severely deteriorated; everyone was suspicious of everyone.

Around 10th May Orwell returned to the front near Huesca. He abandoned his plans to join the International Brigades, who had since become influenced by the communists, because he didn't want

The tower of the Ermita de Salas could be the place where the sniper stood that shot Orwell. The tower still shows the traces of the Civil War[15]

to leave the POUM in the lurch at a time when they were being heavily criticized and because he mistrusted the communists. Kopp's situation was less clear. He may have stayed for longer in Barcelona before returning to Huesca.

Their positions had been slightly moved opposite the Nationalist redoubt, which they had temporarily captured during their raid on 13th April, close to a church named Ermita de Salas. There wasn't much action – the chief trouble was the snipers. The fascist positions were not further than 150 metres away and the trenches of the Republicans were shallow and did not offer a lot of protection. Moreover their positions were lower than the enemy's. All those reasons made Orwell and his companions attractive targets for the snipers operating from the church and the trees. Orwell was tall, 1.93 metres, and that made him an easy target.

At dawn on 20th May, Orwell was hit. Jack Branthwaite, a Scottish working-class volunteer of the ILP contingent, remembered he had just warned him to keep crouched down. According to Frank Frankford, another of Orwell's comrades, he was standing talking about his experiences in a Paris brothel when all of a sudden he fell to the ground, shot in the throat: 'Roughly speaking it was the sensation of being *at the centre* of an explosion. There seemed to be a loud bang and a blinding flash of light all round me, and I felt a tremendous shock – no pain [...]. The next moment my knees crumpled up and I was falling, my head hitting the ground with a violent bang which, to my relief, did not hurt.'[16] Harry Milton, the American, was nearby when he fell: 'He had bitten his lips, so I thought he was a goner.'[17] Milton cut his shirt open to check where he had been hit and helped him onto a stretcher. He was taken to the field hospital of Siétamo, seemingly a lost cause. There he was transported to Barbastro, and from there to Lerida, where he was found by Kopp and Eileen.

Orwell was enormously lucky to have survived, since the bullet had narrowly missed the carotid artery. Kopp managed to see the doctor and sent his report in a detailed letter to Laurence O'Shaughnessy, Eileen's brother. He was a promising surgeon who specialized in the thorax. The letter was written in Barcelona on 10th June in almost flawless English by the French-speaking Kopp: 'The bullet entered the neck just under the larynx, slightly at the left side of it's [sic] vertical axis and went out at the dorsal right side of the neck's base. It was a normal 7mm bore, copper-plated, Spanish Mauser bullet, shot from a distance of some 175 yards. At this range, it still has a velocity of some 600 feet per second and a cauterizing temperature.'[18] The letter also includes a clarifying sketch.

The letter reveals to us an engineer – be it not graduated – who likes to observe meticulously and likes to show off. He even mentions that Orwell's temperature was taken under the left armpit. Impressive, but in-between these rather technical passages we see a different person. He writes that Orwell's sense of humour was unharmed, in itself an illustration of Kopp's own humour. A few lines further he compares his voice with the characteristic, grinding brakes of a very old T-Model Ford. After his stay in Lerida, Orwell was sent to Tarragona, accompanied by Eileen, and after a week he ended up in the Maurin Sanatorium, situated

Maurin Sanatorium, now an international Benjamin Franklin school

in a suburb of Barcelona. Orwell was tired, disillusioned and unsure whether the full use of his voice would return. Still, he applied for a discharge.

On 13th June Kopp fought in what he called the battle of Chimillas, another attempt to take Huesca.[19] This general offensive of the Republicans was launched on 12th June with the intention of cutting off the Jaca road to the west of Huesca and thus isolating the city. The 29th, without Orwell of course, had the task of making diversionary attacks on the Nationalist positions to the north of the city. On 15th June the POUM tried to capture a position called Loma de Los Mártires, but had to withdraw.[20]

On the day Orwell asked for his discharge, probably 14th June, Kopp arrived in Barcelona: 'Full of jubilation. He had just been in action and said that Huesca was going to be taken at last.'[21] Huesca never fell. Months earlier, when Siétamo was occupied, the general commanding the Republican troops had merrily said, 'Tomorrow we will have coffee in Huesca.' It turned out that he was mistaken, and it became a running joke among the militiamen.

On 15th June, when Orwell left to Siétamo to have some documents signed for his discharge, Kopp travelled to Valencia: 'He had a letter from General Pozas, now commanding the Army of the East – the usual letter, describing Kopp as a "person of all confidence" and recommending him for a special appointment in the engineering section.'[22] That must be the time Kopp decided to leave the POUM. The Catalonian army, also called the Army of the East, had been thoroughly reformed after the events of May. It had been professionalized and more Spaniards had taken leading positions. Four International Brigades had been incorporated into the Army of the East under the command of General Pozas. The 29th Division was incorporated into the Spanish regular army.

We do know that the fact that Kopp remained an officer in the new Army of the East is exceptional. The military record of the autodidact Kopp must have been impressive. For safety reasons, before his switch he handed over to John McNair an inventory of the weapons held by the British contingent, along with a map of the 29th Division's positions at the front, but no date is mentioned.[23]

According to documents held in the Archivo General de la Guerra Civil Española in Salamanca, Georges Kopp was a serving officer in the International Brigades. He is listed among the personnel of the brigade general staff (Estado Mayor) in Albacete on both 7th and 17th July, as a captain in the XII Brigade of the 45th Division of the Army of the East, which was under the influence of the communists. We can find his name on a list of 7th July 1937, signed by 'José Vidal' (Vidal Gayman) the base commander, ANGC SM 1061, 925. His name is repeated on a similar list of 17th July 1937 (unfoliated). The XII International Brigade comprised volunteers from Italy and Eastern Europe. He may have been serving in the communications sector.[24] In July Kopp had already been arrested, but that can be explained by the slowly grinding administration mill.[25]

Orwell does mention the trip to Valencia, but not his leaving the POUM, which is very strange. Perhaps Orwell was not aware of Kopp's switch at the time he finished his book in 1938 or he willingly omitted it because at the time it was difficult to make Kopp out as a victim of Stalinism, or else he just wanted to keep things simple for the reader.[26]

Chapter 4

THE REVOLUTION EATS
ITS CHILDREN

On 16th June the Stalinists replaced the left-wing Republican government of Largo Caballero with a more centrist one under Juan Negrín and declared the POUM illegal. Its offices and the Hotel Falcon, where several militiamen stayed, were raided and its newspaper, La Batalla, supressed. The party leader Andrés Nin disappeared and forty prominent party members were arrested. Since the anarchists were also disarmed, the whole left wing was essentially neutralized in a few days.

It took Orwell six days – from 14th to 20th June – to obtain his discharge papers from the 29th Division. He finally managed to return to the Hotel Continental to join Eileen, but there an unpleasant surprise was waiting for him. Eileen met Orwell in the foyer and took him outside; there she told him that the POUM members returning on leave from the front had been disarmed or arrested. Moreover the SIM, the Spanish secret police controlled by the Russian NKVD, had raided their hotel room on 18th June. A guileful Eileen climbed into bed and hid their passports and chequebooks under the sheets. Still, they had lost his diaries, press cuttings, photographs and several letters. Had that not happened his *Homage to Catalonia* would have been an altogether different book. What made Orwell really angry was the arrest of his dear friend Kopp on the very day of his arrival. They decided to destroy his POUM militia card and some incriminating photographs and made plans to escape from Spain.

As mentioned before, Kopp had gone to Valencia to become a captain in the 45th Division of the Army of the East. Kopp can't have been that naïve not to realize he risked being arrested as an ex-POUM commander when he returned to Barcelona on

20th June. An article by David Murray in the *New Leader* of 13th August confirms this:

> After the death of Robert Smillie in Valencia, I spent about a week in the city retrieving his effects and papers.[1] During this period Georges Kopp came to Valencia to obtain a new commission in the Spanish Republican forces. He had been Smillie's commandant in Aragon and naturally came to my hotel to learn some of the details of the sad story.
>
> Just at this time the full report of the Barcelona arrests appeared in the Valencia papers. Georges Kopp was quite aware of the developments in Catalonia, but he told me he had nothing to fear as he was a military commander and had spent most of his time at the front.
>
> I arrived back in Barcelona on Saturday, June 19. The next morning he visited me to deliver two telegrams which had been sent to me at Valencia, but which had been delayed in transmission. One of these messages asked me to suggest to Kopp that he should remain a few days longer in Valencia to complete his business. *This was plainly a warning to him to stay away until his position was regularised.* He showed me, however, a copy of his new commission, appointing him to one of the new divisions forming on the Aragon front, and stating that he was 'a person of every confidence' ... 'una persona de toda confianza'.
>
> I was able to inform him that his room had been searched during his absence, a fact I had learned at the hotel. *He was, however, completely confident that he had never done any conscious wrong against the Spanish Government, and he stated that he had nothing at all of which to be afraid.* He insisted on returning to his quarters, and I accompanied him to the door of the hotel. I learned afterwards that he had been arrested a few minutes after going into his room, since when he has apparently been kept in jail.
>
> Georges Kopp knew of the wave of arrests, he had been warned to stay away from the city, he was aware that his room had been searched. None the less he made no attempt to conceal

his movements. This was an obvious proof that he felt himself innocent, and was, in fact, innocent of any crime against Spain and its legal Government.[2]

He must have thought that no one would stop him while being on an important military mission and having General Pozas's letter of recommendation with him – a capital error of judgement. Just as Orwell shortly after him, he went to the Hotel Continental to get his luggage and there he fell into a trap and was taken to jail. Later that day Eileen and Orwell decided to part and join again at the British Consulate to ask to have their passports put in order so that they could safely leave the country. That night he wandered around until he finally found some sleep in a ruined church. The next day at the consulate they were informed of Bob Smillie's death in unknown circumstances. Smillie had been one of Orwell's fighting pals, so the news upset him intensely and deepened his hate for Stalinists. It would take three days for their passports to be returned, so they decided to visit Kopp in prison. Despite the confusion of mass arrests they could still visit him during the first days, though this would soon change. It took a lot of courage to go there; the risk of being caught was all too realistic. Orwell devoted five pages in his *Homage to Catalonia* to that visit. He wrote it in 1938, but the prose remains remarkably striking:

The so-called jail was really the ground floor of a shop. Into two rooms each measuring about twenty feet square, close on a hundred people were penned. The place had the real eighteenth-century Newgate Calendar appearance, with its frowzy dirt, its huddle of human bodies, its lack of furniture – just the bare stone floor, one bench and a few ragged blankets – and its murky light, for the corrugated steel shutters had been drawn over the windows. On the grimy walls revolutionary slogans – 'Visca POUM!' 'Viva la revolución!' and so forth – had been scrawled. The place had been used as a dump for political prisoners for months past. There was a deafening racket of voices. This was the visiting hour, and the place was so packed with people that it was difficult to move. Nearly all of them were of the poorest of the working-class population. You saw women undoing packets of food which they had brought for their imprisoned men-folk. There were several of the wounded men from the Sanatorium Maurin among the prisoners. Two of them had amputated legs; one of them hopping about on one foot. There was also a boy of not more than twelve; they were even arresting children, apparently. The place had the beastly stench that you always get when crowds of people are penned together without proper sanitary arrangements. Kopp elbowed his way through the crowd to meet us. His plump fresh-coloured face looked much as usual, and in that filthy place he had kept his uniform neat and had even contrived to shave. There was another officer of the popular army among the prisoners. He and Kopp saluted as they struggled past one another; the gesture was pathetic, somehow. Kopp seemed in excellent spirits. 'Well, I suppose we shall all be shot,' he said cheerfully. The word 'shot' gave me a sort of inward shudder. A bullet had entered my own body recently and the feeling of it was fresh in my memory; it is not nice to think of that happening to anyone you know well. At that time I took it for granted that all the principal people in the POUM, and Kopp among them, *would* be shot. The first rumours of Nin's death had just filtered through, and we knew that the POUM were being accused of treachery and espionage. Everything pointed to a huge frame-up trial followed by a massacre of leading 'Trotskyists'. It is a terrible thing to see your friend in jail and to know yourself impotent to help him.'[3]

Still Orwell did not throw in the towel. He gave Kopp some cigarettes and some nourishment, because food in Spanish prisons was terrible. Kopp told him about an important letter which was taken from him during his arrest and which now was at the police headquarters. The letter was destined for the Colonel commanding the military engineering operations of the Army of the East. Both realized that the letter was important to establish Kopp's credibility. Orwell understood that there was only one person who could return the letter: the officer to whom it was addressed. He left Eileen with Kopp and rushed to the Colonel's office at the War Department, which was situated at the harbour. What followed turned out to be a Kafkaesque nightmare. Orwell fought his way through 'hundreds of offices on each floor; and, as this was Spain, nobody has the vaguest idea where the colonel I was looking for was'.[4] Finally he ended up with the Aide-de-Camp of the Colonel, 'a little slip of an officer in smart uniform, with large and squinting eyes', who listened benevolently to his story until the word 'POUM' fell. Cue widespread consternation. To make matters worse Orwell had to admit that he was a Poumista himself. It could easily have been fatal for him, but he was lucky: the Aide-de-Camp did not fall for the story that all members of the POUM were fascist sympathizers. The Aide-de-Camp hurried to the Colonel's office and a heated discussion followed, even by Spanish standards. After some bickering the letter, which was at the police office, finally ended up with the Colonel.

Unfortunately this did not change much and the Colonel did not succeed in securing Kopp's release. The following day Orwell and Eileen visited Kopp for the last time. During the night they strolled aimlessly along the Ramblas and passed the Café Moka, which was still occupied by the Assault Guards. Orwell addressed two guards and one of them remembered Kopp, calling him a 'buen chico' – a nice chap. Orwell realized then that it did not matter whether Kopp was good or bad. They would never let him go, and if he went to trial the Stalinists would deliver falsified, incriminating evidence. Eileen, Orwell and his companions decided to act as 'bourgeois' as possible until they got their passports. They ate expensively, acted especially English with the waiters and frequented the posh quarters of Barcelona where no one knew their faces, but during the night they slept in the open. The strategy worked, and on 23rd June they succeeded in sneaking across the border and escaping from the wasp's nest that the Republicans had created for themselves. Later it became clear that they had been in real danger. In a judiciary record of the trial against the POUM, a 'legajo', dated 13th July 1937, one can read that they were seen as 'rabid Trotskyists' and agents of the POUM.[5] Kopp is mentioned in the document: 'They used to live in the Falcon Hotel supported by the POUM executive committee. / Credential of the POUM executive committee signed by Jorge [sic] Kopp (its nature leads one to suppose that it is a credential which was valid during the events that took place in May) and made out in favour of Eileen B.'[6] How must Kopp have felt? After his failed marriage he sought rehabilitation in battle. He created a new personality and found a new drive. The hero moved swiftly up the military hierarchy and was praised by both friends and enemies. After eight months he fell from his pedestal, not because someone had seen through his lies, but because he had become a plaything in an obscure, ideological battle. Many of his friends escaped the dance and could lick their wounds in their homeland. Kopp, a brilliant talker, was cut off from the outer world. The cosy dinners and drinking parties which he had enjoyed in the middle of wartime vanished. Now he was sinking into oblivion.

With the courage of desperation, he tried to grasp the situation. Letters which he smuggled to the outer world formed his last lifeline. According to Kopp many of them were lost, but fortunately once in a while one found its destination. The letters that were sent from the Hotel Falcon, which had been turned into an unofficial prison, followed a bizarre trail. Kopp had some of them delivered by an Italian antifascist journalist called George Tioli, who also stayed at Hotel Continental and whom Orwell calls 'a great friend of ours'.[7] This slippery character never received these letters because he disappeared around August 1937.[8] A member of the POUM who also worked in the hotel destroyed Tioli's papers, but saw to it that Kopp's letters were sent. A first letter written in English dated 7th July 1937 was addressed to Laurence O'Shaughnessy, Eileen's brother. Kopp asked him to explain his cause through the ILP – he was already aware of the fact that if he did not get in the media he would not exist. The letter was eventually published on 6th August in the *New Leader*. He wrote that he would go on a hunger strike if he did not get an explanation for his arrest within the next forty-eight hours. A second, longer letter written in Spanish, also of 7th July, was destined for Lieutenant-Colonel Burillo. Burillo had communist sympathies, and was head of the police and later security in Barcelona. He was later executed after the change of power in 1939. Kopp complained that his important military mission had been stopped without a clear reason:

I am detained in conditions which are intolerable for any decent individual and in the case of an officer in the Spanish army who has served eight months at the front, amount to an insult. I am mixed with pickpockets, thieves, fascists and homosexuals. I am confined like many of the chief prisoners in a room where there are 18 persons, even though there is room only for three of four. All exercise is denied to us; the food consisting of two plates of soup and two pieces of bread is distributed at unsuitable hours (4 in the afternoon and 11 at night). The guards, although I personally have no cause for complaint, for some of them carry out their duties decently, treat us like cattle, beating the prisoners and insulting them. It appears to me that as a foreign volunteer and officer in the Belgian army, who (after aiding the legal government of Spain by secretly manufacturing munitions in his own country) enlists in the anti-Fascist militia and fights at the front where he successively commands a company, a battalion and a regiment, does not merit this kind of treatment. Nor is such treatment merited by the prisoners I have seen here and who, after weeks of imprisonment, do not know why they have been arrested.[9]

Kopp ends with a remark that the patience of many prisoners may run out. This letter shows that Kopp is eager to impress. He uses long sentences to confirm his intellectual capacity. In the same way, he boasts of his impressive military titles. Still, it is true that someone who has made such a steep climb in military hierarchy in eight months must have lots of potential. We can acknowledge him as a fine fencer with words – praising masterfully and damning discreetly. He never accuses Burillo directly; he pretends to assume that Burillo had already answered an earlier letter, and that the reply had never reached him. And of course he does not mention the word POUM anywhere. He protests in the first place because he is concerned for the fate of his fellow prisoners; if in the process he improves his own fate, so much the better. And he lies blatantly. He had guts to dish up the story of the poor Belgian officer again: Kopp knew that the letter would circulate, and it was almost unavoidable that someone would see through his story. He must have thought that if you lie, you have to keep on lying. After all, he had got away with it thus far. And if Govaerts had not been there, who would have exposed the myth?[10] A third letter on 8th July is to Eileen. You literally feel the despair growing by the day. He writes that he would kill a guard with his bare fists if he was bothered by him. It also becomes clear what was imputed to him: the Assault Guards of Hotel Moka had made false statements claiming that there had been machine guns and other war equipment on the roof of the POUM building that Kopp had defended as commander, and according to them the weapons had been actively used. Still, he would never let go of the sparkle of hope and this enabled him to use humour. Harry Milton, who had served on the Aragon front with the ILP contingent both before and after the 'May Days', was imprisoned with Georges Kopp for a time and helped him out financially, probably to buy food. Kopp writes, 'I promoted him from a gamma minus to an alpha plus status.' That was about the last thing anyone learnt from Kopp during the period of his imprisonment. It did not help one bit that the *New Leader* and *Independent News* asked for his release though their stubbornness was exemplary. The efforts of his comrade-in-arms McNair, who was active in the ILP and had addressed three members of parliament in his party, proved to be useless. A few months later Eileen got to hear from a certain Robert Williams that Kopp was still alive, but that was about it.

An article in the French newspaper *Lutte ouvrière* of 13th August 1937 also turned out to be fruitless. The contribution, titled 'To the militant revolutionaries of all countries' is written in the inflated style of the time and the leftist jargon demands some moderation: 'Heavily indignant we ask you to protest against the reactionary procedures of the liberal bourgeoisie of Spain and its outpost, the Stalinist bureaucracy. [...] Numerous, arbitrarily arrested militants, especially Poumistas, but also anarchists, find themselves in jail. The official press release mentions three hundred arrests among members of the POUM. But one can at least count on a thousand prisoners who have been arrested without reason.' Then a long list of names follows with diverse nationalities. The second name is: 'Georges Kopp – Belgique'. The Germans are only indicated with their initials for fear that family members would be the victims of reprisal under Hitler's rule. The article ends combatively with the motto: 'Free the best fighters against fascism. [...] Long live the proletarian revolution of Europe.' Despite the press campaign Kopp remained imprisoned. More than that, the elapsing of time worked against him. Orwell, Eileen and his fighting pals assumed that if he was not already dead, he soon would be. Alexander Smillie for example, wrote to Eileen that poor Kopp, just as his son, was added to the army of martyrs for the good cause.[11] After a few months Kopp, without knowing, again became the subject of several articles. He was accused of collaboration with the fascists – not unusual, as all members of the POUM got to hear this reproach, except that the attack on Kopp was very specific. On 14th September 1937 the British communist newspaper the *Daily Worker* published the testimony of the earlier mentioned Frank Frankford, who had fought with Orwell and Kopp on the Aragon front. He claimed that each night he and other sentries had heard the rattle of a cart which came from the fascist lines to their positions. They received the command not to shoot on the lights of the cart, and one night near Huesca he had seen commander Kopp returning from the enemy lines. The implication was clear: the cart could have contained food or ammunition and weapons, thus making Kopp a collaborator or a black-marketeer. On 16th December, two days after the publication, he nuanced his allegations: he was not sure that the carts came from the fascist side of the front and he himself had never seen Kopp there. Until 1998 Frankford continued to change his testimonies, but there never came a flat denial. Though no other source offers the irrefutable argument that Kopp did not conspire with the fascists, it is safe to conclude that the story is not plausible.

Jeffrey Meyers, a biographer of Orwell and ardent admirer of Kopp, got to the bottom of the case. In 1937 the Poumista Frank Frankford was arrested in Barcelona on suspicion of receiving stolen paintings and looting churches. Thanks to his childhood friend Lesser, a communist working for the *Daily Worker* as a correspondent, he was released. Lesser fabricated a story to make Kopp, Orwell and consequently the POUM appear in a bad light. Frankford became the benevolent witness because, among other reasons, he loathed Orwell for 'his attack on the English working class' in *The Road to Wigan Pier* (1937). Frankford considered Orwell an elitist and resented the fact that he assumed command of the British contingent, feeling that he never shook his 'policeman' attitude (Orwell had served for five years as a police officer in Burma).[12] One can forgive Orwell's lack of understanding of real 'working-class heroes'; both Orwell and Kopp had studied and both were descendants of an impoverished upper-middle class. But Frankford was not the only one to have the feeling that he was a study object for the writer Orwell. Orwell doubtlessly meant well, but it is impossible to fit in among the workers if you have studied at a posh public school. These sorts of attack from the 'real communists' (i.e., Stalinists) on the POUM can be found everywhere. In his frequently surprising autobiography, David Crook describes how he is recruited by the Russian secret service as a spy to observe Orwell and Kopp, as well as other French and Belgian correspondents of a leftist dissident bent. Espionage and the Spanish Civil War fit hand in glove. The fascists spied on the Republicans, the Republicans on the fascists – especially on their comrades of the Left. No wonder Orwell invented the concept of 'Big Brother'. Crook fitted ideally into that paranoid atmosphere of watching and being watched:

> The Continental Hotel was the hangout of those Britons in Spain who were associated with the Independent Labour Party. They included the ILP's official representative, John McNair, George Orwell, his wife Eileen Blair, and their friend, the Belgian engineer, Major Georges Kopp, portly and middle-aged. Associated with them were writers and journalists including non-communist left-wing correspondents, some from Britain, some from other European countries. I was to become friendly with these people – especially the 'Trotskyists' – get to know their views, activities and contacts, and write reports on them [...].
>
> I recall no significant personal experiences during the fighting itself but I was assigned to play a small part, of which I am not proud, in the crushing of the POUM. I was to go to jail, to be with Georges Kopp and other Poumists, partly to try to glean information from them, partly, no doubt, to confirm my identity as an anti-Stalinist.
>
> About the middle of May the police raided the Continental Hotel in search of incriminating documents in the rooms of such people as Kopp, Eileen Blair and a number of West European (mostly French and Belgian) correspondents of non-communist Left publications or representatives of splinter parties. I was on good terms with these people and when they got wind of the raid (probably when it started on the lower floors of the hotel) helped

them hide papers. I remember balcony scenes in which we flung bundles back and forth so that the rooms would be 'clean' when the searchers entered. A day or so later I was quietly approached by plainclothesmen in the lavatory and hauled off to a makeshift prison. [...]

Kopp was there and he gave me a cordial welcome and found me a place to sleep. This made me uncomfortable. I not only regarded him as an enemy, but disliked him personally. Yet here he was helping me. I have no vivid memories of my ten days inside and recall gathering no intelligence. [...] I did begin to worry after 8 or 9 days, but on the tenth I was escorted upstairs, interrogated by a young Englishman with a nasty wound in the arm, who warned me to behave myself in future and keep better company. I presume he did this on instructions and had no idea as to why I had been hauled in. Again I was in a false position. I felt I was really his comrade, but had to pose as something different.[13]

Some conclusions can be drawn from this chapter of Crook's autobiography. Firstly, his memories are not fully trustworthy. For example, he situates the raid of the Continental Hotel around the middle of May. In reality it happened two days before Kopp's arrest on 20th June. We recognize the naïveté of both the spy and the ones being spied on: no one saw through Crook's 'absurdly thin disguise', least of all Kopp, who gave Crook a warm welcome in jail and helped him to find a place to sleep. It is a pity Crook does not explain why he personally disliked Kopp. Despite this feeling, and with the knowledge he had acquired much later in life, he regrets his actions that helped destroy the POUM.

Crook ended in China, where he fell into disgrace. He was imprisoned during the Cultural Revolution from 1967 until 1973 and rehabilitated by Prime Minister Li Peng, who later was responsible for crushing the student revolt in Tiananmen Square in Beijing. Despite that Crook remained hopeful for China and communism. He died in 1990.

Few historians doubt the innocence of the members of the POUM. In 1937 and 1938 Stalinists organized similar mock trials in Spain as they had done in Russia, in order to monopolize the battle of the Left.[14] They didn't realize that in this way they lost their innocence, thus losing the population's trust.

Then silence fell again. Harry Milton, who was imprisoned with Kopp for some time, was released in August 1937 after pressure from the American Consulate. On his release he sent a letter to Orwell in which he stated that Kopp had been murdered by communists.[15] This was one of the reasons that Orwell completed his *Homage to Catalonia*, which he published on 25th April 1938, with the fearful suspicion that the mouldy labyrinths of secret or semi-secret prisons had swallowed Kopp forever. The knowledge that the SIM, which was strongly influenced by the NKVD, controlled the prisons did not predict anything positive. Even Geert Mak lets Georges Kopp disappear into these dark dungeons in the first editions of his seminal work, *In Europe*.[16] They were all wrong. Kopp was still alive, but that is the only positive thing to be said. For eighteen months two members of the NKVD regularly 'questioned' (i.e., tortured) him, with the help of an interpreter.[17] Luckily Kopp never let on that he knew Russian, as it would have meant the end – a Russian who had joined the POUM was the last thing they would have tolerated.

The goal was to have him sign a declaration in which he admitted that the POUM was a willing instrument in the hands of the fascists. If he pledged allegiance to the Stalinist Communist Party he would be given the rank of lieutenant-colonel.

Kopp's odyssey would take him through innumerable places: first a police station in Barcelona, then to Hotel Falcon, next to premises in Puerta del Ángel, to a clandestine prison in Vallmajor, to a work camp in Segorbe close to Valencia, back to Barcelona, again to Calle Vallmajor, the prison ship *Uruguay*, to a work camp in Falset, to Tamarite (situated in Bonanova, a suburb of Barcelona), to the Palacio de Misiones in Barcelona, back to the *Uruguay*, to the Seminary in Barcelona, the preventorium of Colell and again to the Seminar.[18]

His circumstances varied from cramped prisons, to damp caverns, to work camps. He suffered twenty-seven interrogations during 135 hours in Puerta del Ángel and was locked up for twelve days in a coal shed without light or air, little water and no food, unless he

The prison near Puerta del Ángel 24 has become a branch of Zara

caught the enormous rats which darted over his legs. The first person to see Kopp after his solitary confinement barked that he would shoot him the very same evening.

The result was a weight loss of 44 kilos, scars, blood poisoning and scurvy. Forget the pictures of the corpulent, blushing Kopp: seventeen prisons later, all that remained was a meagre shadow, plodding along with the help of a walking cane.

Kopp added to his file that the Russians were keen on an anti-tank weapon which was designed by him and was supposed to have been tested on the Valencia front. There is no evidence of such a prototype; certainly Peter Davison, the authority on the life and works of Orwell, is doubtful of its existence.[19]

On 16 November 1938 his mother Henriette Neimann wrote to the Belgian secret service to plead for her son. In the letter she gives two addresses: Campo de Trabajo nr. 6, Pueblo Espagnol, Montjuic and the prison ship *Uruguay*, both in Barcelona.[20] She asks for written permission to allow her son to enter Belgium again, and adds that he had never been politically active or a member of an organization. He is Russian, because 'he failed to fulfil the necessary formalities to become a Belgian'.[21] The secret service replied they would have no objection to him entering Belgium again.

In his 2010 article, 'The Spies Who Loved Them', Rob Stradling claims that Kopp may have been working for the PSUC, the pragmatic communists of Catalonia under influence of Russia. Although Stradling frequently uses scientific methods and data, his conclusions are dubious as he is too selective in his arguments.

Let us focus on the Kopp case: "Is it possible, then, not that the Blairs failed to save Kopp, but that Kopp succeeded in saving the Blairs? Or even that Eric and Eileen were actually saving themselves in the very actions they took in order to rescue Kopp? By the time that Kopp came to live in Britain, in 1939, it seems that his friendship with Eric had already faded." Stradling claims that despite his later marriage to Doreen Hunton, Eileen's sister-in-law, and Kopp's later successful activities as an MI5 intelligence agent, the two men did not meet again, probably because Eric realized that Kopp had been interested in his wife rather than in him.

"Quite contrary to what Blair believed and Orwell's readers have accepted to date, Kopp may have been present in PSUC prisons as a stool-pigeon, in order to inform on his fellow-prisoners." Stradling accuses Kopp of having been a spy for the communists in prison because he finds it difficult to believe that Kopp had to stay in jail while others, such as Josep Rivera, who had been in similar circumstances had been released. Stradling sees other anomalies which could be explained by Kopp being a communist spy.

To give some examples: Kopp's handing over to John McNair (apparently for safe keeping) an inventory of the weapons held by the British section of the POUM militia, along with a map of the 29th Division's positions at the front; his knowledge of the impending fate of the POUM as a whole; his ability to negotiate a local truce with the Civil Guards next door to the Hotel Falcon during the 'May Events'; above all, his ability to survive the subsequent purge, seemingly suffering no serious ill effects from a lengthy period of (mentally and physically) punitive custody.[22]

According to Stradling, Kopp being a stool pigeon had made it possible for the Blairs to escape. As a communist spy, he had simply allowed them to. The efforts of the *Daily Worker* and Frankford to blacken Kopp's reputation would have been parts of a disinformation campaign to make his cover as an anti-Stalinist and pro-Trotskyite even more convincing.

However, Stradling uses too many conjectures. To name one: he writes that Orwell and Kopp did not meet again, which is manifestly wrong, as the reader will discover in the next chapters. They met several times before Orwell's death. The suggestion that Kopp survived his imprisonment relatively unharmed is also absurd. This too will be refuted in the next chapters. Suffice to say that his daughter Anne-Marie hardly recognized him when she met him in Brussels after his release.

Stradling's article would fit into Orwell's *Nineteen Eighty-Four*. It is easy to rewrite history: use real data and sources and mix them with conjecture and the reader may believe you in the end. Kopp was accused of collaborating with the fascists; now he is supposed to have been a PSUC spy. Based on trustworthy sources we can assume relatively safely that Kopp was a member of POUM, transferred to the International Brigades, but was arrested by the SIM because of his past.

Chapter 5

WEIN, WEIB UND GESANG[1]

During Orwell's recovery Kopp often visited him. If they weren't at the front both preferred to observe women, if possible from a terrace. Kopp certainly wasn't less mesmerized by the fairer sex than Orwell – adultery was, after all, the reason for his divorce. The *epith. ornans* 'weaker sex' was consequently more applicable to him than to women. A passage from Kopp's letters illustrates this. Orwell is convalescing in the Sanatorium Maurin: 'Today is the thirtieth of May. Eric travelled on his own initiative by tram and metro to the centre of Barcelona, where I met him at a quarter to twelve. He explained his escapade by the need of cocktails and a proper lunch.' Perhaps this says more of Orwell, but Kopp gives himself away at the end of the letter: 'Most nurses are brunettes.'

We can safely conclude that as far as women are concerned, Orwell and Kopp were two of a kind. Did that have implications for the relationship between them and Eileen, Orwell's wife?

Eileen O'Shaughnessy married Orwell on June 1936 at the age of 29 and consequently dropped her studies in psychology. Friends described her as witty, lively, intelligent and charming. Photos show the type of girl that would be described in the 1930s as 'handsome'. She has something of a Hollywood star about her, but without the glitter and with a distant look. Her friend Lady Violet Powell remembered her 'heart-shaped face' and 'Irish colouring'.[2] Her letters reflect the sardonic sense of humour which appealed to Orwell and Kopp. She writes that a few months after her wedding, 'I lost my habit of punctual correspondence during the first few weeks of my marriage because we quarrelled so continuously & bitterly that I thought I'd save time & just write one letter to everyone when the murder or separation had been accomplished.'[3] She admits that both her husband and she herself were impossible to live with.

Although some friends called her defensive and curiously elusive, one could doubt whether she was so difficult to live with. In the nine years prior to her death she supported Orwell in everything he undertook. As you can expect from a man whose books changed the world, everything, including a relationship, was sacrificed for his literary career. Moreover his love was not exclusively for her, as his shopping list of mistresses would attest to. Because of Orwell's lung problems they rented a villa in the mild Marrakech region, with money given to them by a patron, in the winter of 1938 to 1939.[4] He became fascinated by the Berber girls of the Atlas Mountains, finding it impossible to resist their ogling eyes, tattooed bodies and pointed breasts, and eventually Eileen agreed that he could go ahead and indulge himself.[5]

You could not say she had been ignorant of his weaknesses before they married. She once confided to her brother Laurence that Orwell, contrary to Laurence, would not have travelled to the other end of the world if she had asked him to, though she did so for him. She followed him to Spain and supported him when he returned from the front, utterly exhausted. As previously discussed, she even came to see him at the front.

In the picture below we can see Eileen behind a wall of sandbags, in between the Poumistas. Everyone is wearing all kinds of things: boots, corduroy trousers, puttees, jumpers and berets, in other words anything but a uniform. Orwell is standing in the centre of the picture, towering above the others and the parapet; it's not surprising that he would be shot through the throat later. Eileen is sitting next to him. In front of the picture a man is demonstrating in a peculiar way how to use a Hotchkiss machine gun, model 1914. To the extreme right, the joker of the party is holding a cooking pot above his head. I'd like to think Kopp took the photograph, because he probably accompanied Eileen during her three days' stay. We know for sure that he took her back to Barcelona.

Did they have an affair? A letter to her close friend Norah Miles sheds some light on what Eileen herself calls the 'Dellian' (i.e., Delian – that is, difficult) situation she had landed in with Kopp. The letter was written in early January 1938, and Kopp had not yet been released from prison.[6] She writes that Kopp was more than 'a bit gone' on her during her stay in Spain. Only when back in Great Britain did Orwell discover that Kopp had been in love with his wife, when he accidentally

Far left is John Braithwaite, third from the left (kneeling) is the American Harry Milton, fourth from the left (looking down) is Charles Justessen and then Philip Hunter. Next to him is Reg Hiddlestone, the tall man next to him is George Orwell. Eileen O'Shaughnessy is sitting to the right of Orwell. Second from the right is John Agnew. The machine gun is a Hotchkiss Model 1914. Orwell Archive, UCL Special Collections.

opened one of Kopp's letters. It cannot be proven they ever did more than hold each other's hands, but certain passages are quite suggestive:

> *I sometimes think no one ever had such a sense of guilt before. It was always understood that I wasn't what they call in love with Georges – our association progressed in little leaps, each leap immediately preceding some attack or operation in which he would almost inevitably be killed, but the last time I saw him he was in jail, waiting, as we were both confident, to be shot, and I simply couldn't explain to him as a kind of farewell that he could never be a rival to George. So he has rotted in a filthy prison for more than six months with nothing to do but remember me in my most pliant moments. If he never gets out, which is indeed most probable, it's good that he has managed to have some thoughts in a way pleasant, but if he does get out I don't know how one reminds a man immediately after he is a free man again that one has only once missed the cue for saying that nothing on earth would induce one to marry him.[7]*

The word 'pliant' is especially intriguing; I will leave it to the reader to interpret.

According to Eileen, Orwell's opening of the letter hadn't changed his attitude towards Georges Kopp. This will surprise no one, because Orwell wasn't the jealous type. He said many times that he didn't care who was sleeping with whom. He ranked intellectual and emotional loyalty above sexual faithfulness. So Orwell didn't mind: 'He is very fond of Georges, who indeed cherished him with real tenderness in Spain and anyway is admirable as a soldier because of his remarkable courage, and he is extraordinarily magnanimous about the whole business – just as Georges was extraordinarily magnanimous. Indeed they went on saving each other's lives or trying to in a way that was almost horrible to me, though George had not then noticed.'[8]

Although Eileen kept on fighting for Kopp's release she had clearly put the Spanish period behind her: 'On the whole it's a pity I found that letter because Spain doesn't really dominate us as much as all that.'[9] She then continues about their nineteen hens and their breeding pen. In an attempt to create distance she asked him to send his letters to her brother Laurence so that he could then forward them to her. This didn't stop Kopp using phrases such as, 'Tell her how intensely I think of her, give her my love and give Eric a hand.'

We can safely say that Eileen and Kopp did not have a long-lasting affair, but she certainly was not insensitive towards Kopp's advances in Spain. And although he was no *beau garçon*, he seemed to have a way with women. His charm, sense of humour and boyish enthusiasm did the trick. According to Rosalind Obermeyer, Eileen's eyes lit up at the mention of Kopp.[10] All the circumstances were there to give in to short-term temptations. They lived intense lives and death was lurking behind every corner. On top of it all Eileen didn't have a lot to do, so a suitor was a welcome distraction: 'Certainly she had been caught up in the war atmosphere and the whirl of café life in Barcelona. As she told her mother, "I have coffee about three times a day & drinks oftener [...]. Every night I mean to go home early & write letters or something & every night I get home the next morning."'[11] Kopp wasn't the only interested man during Eileen's Barcelona days and nights: 'Men had gathered around Eileen like suitors around Homer's Penelope: not only O'Donnell, but also Georges Kopp,

Giorgio Tioli, David Wickes and David Crook, to name only five.'[12] Of these, Crook was spying on the Blairs and on Kopp, and he wrote in his reports that he was '95 per cent certain that Kopp and Eileen were on intimate terms'.[13]

Kopp probably hadn't had a woman for months, so the rustling of skirts and the soft inclination of the bosom must have had a compelling impact. And they had plenty of opportunity, since Kopp made several visits to Barcelona on military business while his men, particularly Orwell, remained at the front.[14] We can conclude that if they had had a short-lived affair it didn't affect their bond, so the question becomes irrelevant. George, Georges and Eileen supported one another through thick and thin.

Chapter 6

FREE AT LAST

On 7th December 1938 Kopp was released because, according to him, the Belgian government had put pressure on the Republican government behind the scenes. It is possible of course, but we must not forget Kopp was no Belgian citizen. In his MI5 file (which will be dealt with later) Kopp used Spaak, former Belgian minister of foreign affairs, in exile in London, as a reference. When this was checked, Spaak stated that 'he could remember nothing about Kopp. The name struck no chord in his memory.'[1] This is in line with the story as told by Bob Edwards, commander of the ILP contingent in Spain, who had served under Kopp. Edwards admired Kopp, but even he had to admit that Kopp sometimes exaggerated:

> I suppose I knew Georges Kopp better than any other person. We lived and worked together during the Spanish Civil War on the Aragon front for three months […]. Georges Kopp was one of the many courageous men who came to Spain to fight because fighting was a kind of a career for them […]. He was inclined to exaggerate. For example he told me he was a friend of Henry Spaark [Paul-Henri Spaak], the Socialist Foreign Minister of Belgium, and I discussed the plight of Georges Kopp with him and indeed it was Spaark's intervention that had Georges Kopp released from prison. But Spaark denied any knowledge of Georges Kopp, and as far as I am aware, he had no background of activity in the Labour Movement of Belgium.[2]

We can conclude that the Belgian Ministry of Foreign Affairs may have used some influence to obtain Kopp's release, but certainly not Spaak in person.

Was that decisive or were there other factors which led to his release? Was it the publication of Kopp's letters in the newspapers or the efforts of the ILP? Or was it because he had threatened to make two incriminating files of the SIM public?

Kopp claimed that he had stolen these files while imprisoned, and refers to them in letters which he wrote to Orwell and Eileen in January 1939. What he wrote exhales paranoia. He felt spied on and did not want to be (atypical for him) at the centre of attention. He longed for rest and was exhausted:

> *My room is not safe, it has already been searched twice and they have been at my mother's to bother her [...]. My health bothers me too; the night before last I have had trouble with the old heart and could not sleep even a moment; yesterday when having lunch at a friend's, I collapsed and had to stay all the afternoon in a settee. It is very annoying and I feel helpless when what the Spaniards call the 'hermano cuerpo' [human body] is not keeping pace with the still alert mind.*[3]

The letters with a summary of the stolen files mainly deal with Marc Rein and Bob Smillie, but also with Gaston Weil and Georges Chenais, all foreigners in Spanish prisons.[4] Bob Smillie was the grandson of a known mining union leader, who had fought with Orwell and Kopp and who died during captivity in mysterious circumstances. Smillie's file was addressed to Fenner Brockway and John McNair of the ILP; Orwell received a copy of all the letters.

The letters read as thrillers. The abundance of details, typical of his writing style, makes them instantly recognizable. When he was arrested he was taken to the headquarters of the secret police at Puerta del Ángel 24 in Barcelona. It used to be a jewellery store, consisting of a cellar which functioned as a garage, a ground floor with offices and several floors with cells and interrogation rooms: 'I was brought into the garage on July 21st 1937 and, from the beginning, managed to make contact with the POUM people outside. A regular system of letter-carrying was established by means of the windows looking onto the mews.'[5] During his first routine interrogation he noticed two files bearing the names of Bob Smillie and Marc Rein. Time went on and after some weeks he claims he saw three prisoners being led to the sub-cellar under the garage and heard shots. Afterwards he saw the dead bodies being taken away on stretchers.

Since he had nothing to lose, on the night of 28th September he burgled the office where he had seen the files, while the sentries were asleep. He stole them, made a parcel and had it smuggled to George Tioli, but as mentioned before the parcels and Tioli disappeared. Luckily he had gone, be it swiftly, through the files so that he was able to report that Marc Rein had been shot and that Bob Smillie had died of brutal mistreatment.

Certainly the case of Smillie is controversial, even now. David Murray, representative of the ILP, investigated the case on the spot and came to the conclusion that Bob Smillie had died die to a combination of peritonitis and gross negligence of the prison staff. The ILP accepted this version because it did not want any political debate. If Smillie had died directly through torture, the leftist ILP would have had to have called the leftist Republican government to account, and that was a sensitive matter.

It remains strange that no one took Kopp seriously; in his letter to the ILP he reports the facts so minutely and nuanced that it takes an effort not to believe it. The following passage concerns the doctor's report:

The doctor states that Bob had the skin and the flesh of his belly perforated by a powerful kick delivered by a foot shod in a nailed boot; the intestines were partly hanging outside. Another blow had severed the left side connection between the jaw and the skull and the former was merely hanging on the right side. Bob died about 30 minutes after reaching the hospital and nothing could be done to save him, although they gave him plenty of morphia to alleviate the pain.[6]

Moreover he gives the names of other witnesses, which could easily have been checked after 1938. But Kopp's testimonies were words in the wind. As far as we know from written sources, Orwell, the ILP and Bob Smillie's parents never acted on the letters.

Not until 1998 did anyone stand up to defend Kopp. John Newsinger of the University of Bath found his testimony credible and did not understand why Tom Buchanan, a scholar of the University of Oxford, would not take that into account in his article about Smillie.[7] Buchanan wipes Kopp's report from the table, because he does not regard him as a reliable witness.[8] Not surprising: Buchanan quotes, among others, Govaerts, Davison and Shelden to undermine Kopp's credibility.[9]

According to Govaerts, Kopp's release had nothing to do with efforts of Spaak, the ILP or his files. It is more likely that his interrogators were so impressed by the fierce Spanish and foreign reactions on the disappearance of Andrés Nin that they decided to cease killing Poumistas. The authors André Gide, André Malraux, François Mauriac and many others pushed for a fair trial. During the hearings Kopp was mentioned a few times without much effect. Everyone stayed in jail. The judges pronounced a very strange verdict. They acquitted the Poumistas of espionage, but condemned several leaders to harsh prison sentences for slander of the Catalonian government. When Kopp was of no further use he was released.

According to Kopp he then flew from Barcelona to Toulouse.[10] There he sent a telegram to Orwell to say that he was saved but in a bad state. Then he went to Paris where he was received by a delegation of the POUM and Marceau Pivert, the leader of the small, leftist Parti Socialiste Ouvrier et Paysan. Somewhat later he wrote to Orwell to sketch his journey in the underworld. He also asked if Orwell could see to it that the ILP sent him £50.

He probably arrived in Brussels on 31st December – his daughter Anne-Marie remembers waiting for her father at the station around that time.[11] She thinks that there was also a delegation of Belgian socialists on the platform. Anne-Marie thought he had been hit between a hammer and anvil when she finally saw him after two years. He looked worn out and literally half the man he had been.[12] He did not stay there for long and soon returned to Paris. On 10th January he let Orwell know how grateful he was towards him:

I see I have completely forgotten to thank Eric for the steps taken in my favour in the early days of my imprisonment. You have been splendid Eric, and I really do admire you for what you did when you were in hiding, approaching major's Fenech Secretary [sic], the Police headquarters and those Assault Guards in the Moka; it was daring and it would have been 100% nice if it had succeeded in keeping me out of trouble. In any case, it was awfully brave and some sort of heroical [sic]. [...] When shall we see us again, my

dear friends? [...] You are the only ones sufficiently befriended and aware of
Spain to understand what I have been through and to 'mother' me a little...[13]

Kopp was understandably bitter because he felt he had suffered for a cause he no longer believed in. Orwell will have understood him perfectly, for in a letter to Heppenstall he wrote: 'To think that we started off as heroic defenders of democracy and only six months later were Trotsky-Fascists sneaking over the border with the police at our heels.'[14]

It was clear that Kopp longed for his friends Orwell and Eileen. He thought of joining them in Great Britain, where he felt safer than on the Continent. The problem was that they were in Morocco during that time and, judging from her letter to Norah Myles of mid-December 1938, Eileen clearly was not very keen on having him there: 'George Kopp proposes to come & stay with us (he has no money & we had heard the day before by cable that he was out of jail & Spain; Eric's reaction to the cable was that George must stay with us & his reaction to George's letter announcing his arrival is that he must *not* stay with us, but I think the solution may be that George won't find anyone to lend him the necessary money).'[15]

It is quite understandable that they did not want to spend their journey with a third party. Both had put the Spanish episode behind and wanted to move on. And Orwell was right – he never made it to Morocco for lack of money. It also proves that Eileen no longer had strong feelings for him. That did not stop them taking care of Kopp, as by the end of January they had made arrangements for him to stay with Laurence and Gwen O'Shaughnessy at 24 Crooms Hill in Greenwich, London.[16] As they were both doctors they could offer the ideal place to convalesce. Laurence was already a renowned surgeon by then. Kopp gained strength and among others got to know Doreen Hunton, the younger half-sister of Gwen. She was eight years younger than him and would later become his wife.

On 5th March 1939, while they were staying in Morocco, Orwell wrote to Jack Common, an inhabitant of the small cottage in Wallington where Orwell and Eileen lived. Orwell asked Jack to pretend as if he invited Kopp to stay in a house near the cottage, while it was in fact Orwell. He was worried that things might turn out too hectic at the O'Shaughnessy's, because they had just had a baby. Gwen would pay for the costs of his stay, but it was very important that he think he was Jack's guest. Orwell did not suppose it would cause problems:

> *You may remember reading in my book on the Spanish war about Georges Kopp, who was commander of my brigade for a while. [...] I think you'll like him also. Of course this might turn out not to be necessary, some job might turn up for him in the mean while, but I doubt whether he's fit to work yet after being 18 months in jail and starved and so forth. [...] He is quite handy in the house & adores cooking. [...] He's the sort of man who's happy anywhere if people are pleased to see him & you'd find him interesting to talk to – he speaks English quite fluently.*[17]

We know that Kopp did not accept the invitation, perhaps because he did not feel like living without luxuries in the relative loneliness of the countryside. Thus Orwell's plan failed.

During his stay in Great Britain, Kopp wrote 'Petit essai d'analyse Marxiste des événements d'Espagne 1936–1939'.[18] The essay was going to serve as an introduction to the French edition of Orwell's *Homage to Catalonia*. It took so long for the French translation to be published that Orwell or his editor chose not to include it after all. Somehow the times had changed and the jargon and contents had become outdated. Kopp conceived the essay as a kind of chronological overview of the Spanish Civil War. It is striking that contrary to other writings this essay of eleven typed pages does not contain any reflection on his personal situation.

It is hard to judge the essay on its veracity and its originality. Here and there one recognizes Orwellian thoughts: 'But the triumphant proletariat makes a fundamental mistake: it does not destroy this machine [the bourgeoisie] but places a new apparatus under it, the Committees, and it invites the old rulers of Spain to collaborate, if they show an anti-Fascist attitude.'[19] Orwell, too, wrote that the bourgeoisie had never left Barcelona. They lied doggo until they had the occasion to be in power again.

In the essay he stays loyal to the principles which the POUM endorsed, because according to him the Republican jailers knew that the accusations of collaboration with the enemy were fabricated. They granted him a relative freedom in prison. Even the fascists realized that they – not the communists – were the true revolutionaries.

Kopp did not think highly of Negrín, the leader of the Republicans, in the last phase of the war, for it was he who banned the POUM and brought the Spanish Left under Russian influence. It went wrong because the workers' movement did not stay loyal to the revolutionary doctrine. What the doctrine comprised he leaves unexplained. He concludes his essay as follows: 'Let us draw lessons from the Spanish drama that it at least leads to the proletariat's better understanding of the conditions of battle. [...] Let us have faith in ourselves, but on condition that we have earned it through a thorough study of our past, through a clear view of our duties. We shall succeed.'[20]

As do all human beings, Kopp evolved his thought. Later he moved to the centre and warned his daughter Anne-Marie of the dangers of communism and of historical materialism in particular.[21] According to Anne-Marie, he referred to his essay to show that he had studied Marxism exhaustively. This is questionable, as we cannot find any digression on this in his writing.

This pretence was typical of Kopp – according to Anne-Marie he could get away with almost everything. Once, during a reception, a doctor of medicine had asked Anne-Marie if her father was a doctor too, because he managed to converse in medical jargon seemingly without effort.

In May 1939 he left for Paris to work as a consulting engineer with M. Chenais, a former client of his.

Chapter 7

'I WANT TO LIVE GRAND AND GLORIOUSLY'[1]

In September 1939 Kopp realized that he could no longer escape from his old demon: fascism. He tried to join the French army and ended up in the French Foreign Legion. The legionnaires are still regarded as elite troops, or if you prefer: the cannon fodder of the military. The officers are French, but the soldiers come from all over the world and it was tacitly accepted that volunteers were often desperate people looking for a new identity. Kopp falls outside this category, but if he wanted to fight against the German troops, he did not have many options.

He likely underwent a period of training first and was later assigned to the 12th Regiment, formed on 25th February 1940. It consisted of a hotchpotch of beaten Spanish Republicans and Polish, German and Austrian refugees, including quite a few Jews, all of whom needed little motivation to fight against the German fascists. Because the army command assembled this regiment later than most, they didn't all have the current uniforms, so the regiment was dependent on what was left over. On 30th April they were ready for combat, but without the promised 25mm anti-tank cannons. Nothing new for Kopp, who now was a corporal and leader of a battle group of the first company. The entire 12th Regiment was commanded by Lieutenant-Colonel Besson, an able and energetic officer who came with ornate decorations from World War I. On 11th May, the 12th Regiment was added to the 8th Infantry Division, and was given a baptism of fire.

To give a brief overview: Hitler invaded Poland on 1st September 1939. The Germans developed their blitzkrieg. The British and French, both of which guaranteed the integrity of the Polish territory, declared war on Germany. Owing to a secret clause in the

Cet extrait est à plier en deux par le milieu de façon à ce que l'inscription soit à l'intérieur.

Art. 24 du Règlement
Format : 11,5 x 16,5

EXTRAIT DU LIVRET INDIVIDUEL

NOM KOPP   Classe : 1939

Prénoms : Georges   Grades   2 classe / Caporal

N° d'incorporation : 87879   successifs

Corps ou Service   Dépôt Commun des Régiments Étrangers d'Infanterie.

Unités successives { CR2, C46, C.P.1

Signature du Commandant d'unité et cachet du Chef de corps

SIGNALEMENT
Cheveux Blonds clairs
yeux Gris Verts
front Ordinaire
nez Fort
visage Ovale
Renseig. physionomiques con
taille 1.74.
Marques particulières :

À plier ici

CHANGEMENT DE CORPS

Passé le 1er Avril 1940.
au 12e R E I. 1e Compagnie
comme Caporal.
nouveau n° d'incorporation 87879.

Passé le
au
comme
nouveau n° d'incorporation

Passé le
au
comme
nouveau n° d'incorporation

Signature des Commandants d'Unité

NOTA IMPORTANT. — Le présent extrait ne donne droit au tarif militaire sur les chemins de fer que s'il est présenté conjointement avec une feuille de route ou un des titres qui suppléent cette pièce (ordre de route, sauf conduit, congé, permission ou ordre de service).

IMP DU PROGRES BEL-ABBES

non-aggression pact between Germany and the Soviet Union, the Soviet troops attacked Poland on 17th September. The country was quickly overrun and divided between Hitler and Stalin. Hitler, temporarily freed from the Soviet threat, could now concentrate on the Western Front. Nevertheless, large-scale military land operations failed to occur for the time being. It was a 'Phoney War'. On 9th April 1940 German troops invaded Denmark and Norway without warning and cut the Allies off at the pass in their effort to control railroads and shipping routes. A French–British Expeditionary Force still intervened in Narvik (Norway), but because of the situation in France the corps was recalled in late May. As of 10th May, Belgium, the Netherlands, Luxembourg and France were affected by the blitzkrieg themselves. The German air force provided the necessary support to the advance of the armour which marched to the sea through the north of France. The Allied armies were thus cut in half. A huge wave of refugees flooded the roads. The Dutch and Belgian armies capitulated after a struggle of five and eighteen days respectively, and the British withdrew what remained of their expedition army from Dunkirk. Thus France was left entirely on its own and had to retreat with a large loss of troops and material, while the German forces retained their combat power.

Yet the situation was not hopeless for France; the country had large reserves and the German numerical superiority was still not overwhelming. But this potential was not fully harnessed and the army squandered major armoured reserves in futile attacks on German bridgeheads over the Somme. Too many of the units remained behind the Maginot Line and insufficient emergency units were formed.[2]

Therefore it was high time to throw the 12th Regiment into the battle. The plan was to concentrate around Meaux, and later Chateau-Thierry, east of Paris, but due to transport problems it took several days before the regiment reached its destination. The first victims fell through air raids. The legionnaires had to defend a stretch of twelve kilometres and seven bridges over the Aisne in the region of Soissons. This they tried by counter-attacking on the night of 5th June to 6th June near Malmaison. It was only a reprieve, as the German Stukas, artillery and tanks hit back so hard that the French only managed to retain their advanced positions for ten hours and suffered major losses.

On 6th June Lieutenant-Colonel Besson resolved to defend the bridges at all costs, but on the following day resorted to blowing them up in an attempt to stop the Germans. That worked briefly, but during the night of 7th and 8th June, they had to retreat under heavy enemy fire. The departments still working with horses and carts endured the worst of the slaughter.

The days that followed were a repeat of the same scenario: retreating to the south and resisting in vain at every stream. On 9th and 10th June they fought near Neuilly-Saint-Front at the river Ourcq, on 11th and 12th June in Nanteuil-sur-Marne, 12th and 13th June in Villaret-Bussières at the Grand Morin, 14th June in Bray-sur-Seine, and on 15th June in Montereau-Fault-Yonne. It is a retreat of about 110 kilometres – as the crow flies – in ten days.

Kopp took part in this disastrous campaign from 6th June onwards. The poor French motorized infantry divisions were not able to retreat flexibly, so unit by unit they were separated. This all-out war must have shocked him, especially since he had hardly put his traumatic experiences in Spanish prison behind him.

On 15th June he was wounded by enemy fire, and we know quite precisely under what circumstances, because on 17th December 1941 he wrote a letter to George and Evelyn, whom he met when he stayed with Laurence and Gwen O'Shaughnessy.[3] That the letter ended up in his MI5 file may seem surprising, but it is an important document:

> *In June '40 I have been wounded on the Yonne; I got 4 rifle bullets through the right lung; the left hand, the left elbow and in the left collarbone. I got hit during a short but not rearguard* [unreadable word]. *The bullets, shot at some 30 yards, were not enough* [i.e., did not have enough speed] *to preserve their cauterizing properties so that no secondary trouble arose. I must say that the chap who fired at me at so short a range without killing me was a very bad shot indeed; I managed to get one of his fellows down, and then – although wounded – another one; I wouldn't get the man who was arming* [aiming] *at me because he took cover behind the wheels of a lorry of some sorts. When blood loss and the damage to my left hand prevented me from going on firing from the village pavement where I was alone (I was coming back from a liaison mission when the Germans drove into the village). They came and sort of picked me up; I was brought to a sanitary formation for prisoners of war; whence I managed to escape as soon as my health permitted me to limp and walk i.e. after two months, the 16th of August 1940. I got back to the regiment who did splendidly through the whole show.*[4]

The military hospital was Hôpital Bégin in Saint-Mandé near Paris, and still exists today. In an earlier letter to Eileen on 8th September 1940 he describes the situation in the hospital. Because of the appalling conditions seven hundred patients were soon reduced to three hundred. Especially for Eileen's brother, a surgeon specialized in the thorax, he mentions how the patients are anesthetized by kicking them in their solar plexus.[5]

The engineer in him scrutinizes the speed of bullets, but Kopp never lost his bravado and his black humour, witnessed by his reference to the war as a 'show' and his critique of his assailant as 'a very bad shot'. It seems lifted from a cheap adventure movie: the hero lands in trouble, defends himself bravely, is imprisoned and escapes despite serious injury. We have no other witnesses; perhaps he exaggerated, perhaps not, but it remains a good story. In any case, his confrontation fits seamlessly into the many records of other soldiers. This was no conflict with modern, collateral damage, but a dirty, total war of man-to-man battles and bayonets. At the end of the campaign two-thirds of the 12th Regiment was eliminated. Germany signed an armistice on 22nd June in France. The Germans occupied the northern part of the country; the south-east was governed as the so-called neutral state of Vichy – in fact a puppet regime of Nazi Germany.

So Kopp escaped on 16th August 1940 and joined his unit in Fuveau, Bouches-du-Rhône, not far from Marseilles, where he was first nominated for the croix de guerre and médaille militaire awards. This wasn't to be as two others in his unit had already received them. He was then nominated for the Légion d'honneur, but whether he actually received knighthood is unknown. He writes in the aforementioned letter to George and Evelyn that he is 'speaking of these trifles because of Eileen who sort of wrote that he was wishing me to get some medals in the war'. The 'he' must be Orwell.

He writes to Eileen that he was considering joining the Free French, De Gaulle's government in exile, set up in London as a counterweight against the Vichy regime. Kopp must have had it difficult in a relatively calm period from late August to early September. He extols the French countryside and the 'brioches au chocolat' lifestyle, mainly because he hopes that he will one day share them with Eileen. Whether Orwell can join her isn't stated in so many words. He not only misses his children but his English friends, Eileen in particular; he isn't successful with the local women. He adds bitterly that the Germans seduce them all, since 'the woman is the reward of the victor'. The letter is lyrically written, especially the end: 'Do I have to tell you what joy it will be for me to see you and hear everyone in the family to see who I hope they make it up. You know all that. You even know what "Pensées choisies" I send you. With love, George.'

The term 'Pensées choisies' (chosen thoughts) is mainly used in the later letters to his daughter; it was his formula to indicate that they had a bond – he reserved special thoughts for them. He clearly cherished Eileen, but it would be a bridge too far to suggest she was the love of his life. Perhaps he was lonely and missed his friends. Kopp wrote in what the English call a 'continental' style: his Russian nature meant that he was less inclined to hide his feelings and he had a tendency to gush.

In September 1940 he was transferred to the depot of the Foreign Legion in Sidi Bel Abbès in north-western Algeria. In December 1940 or February 1941 he received an honourable discharge because of permanent injuries to his left lung and left hand, with a disability pension of eighty per cent, representing 400 French francs per month.[6] His left hand was of little use because his thumb had been amputated and two fingers were paralysed. During his stay in Algeria he probably caught malaria, and a cocktail of disease and disability was created which would significantly shorten his life. The only advantage was that the malaria made Kopp 'immune against syphilis, which in my case is a great thing'.[7]

Chapter 8

IN SERVICE OF A PUPPET GOVERNMENT

In Sidi Bel Abbès Kopp got to know Captain Daigny, who officially served in the Foreign Legion but in reality was head of the Deuxième Bureau, the French intelligence service. Daigny recognized the potential in Kopp and proposed that he work for the French admiralty. The aim was to secretly start up a production of synthetic oil which could be used by the French naval force of the Vichy regime. As previously mentioned, Kopp initially wanted to go to his friends in Great Britain to continue the battle against fascism there, but during the winter he caught a fever and suffered chest pains, which made him realize that the true soldier's life was no longer for him. He accepted Daigny's proposal and left for Marseille. Contradictions and Kopp go hand in hand: first he wanted to join General De Gaulle's Free French Forces in London, then a month later he dedicated himself to the adversary, the Vichy regime.

Kopp's dream was to produce synthetic oil massively and profitably, in order to solve his financial problems once and for all. Oil is of enormous strategic importance, and countless military offensives have stalled owing to the lack of fuel. If a party managed to manufacture synthetic oil on a large scale, it would have an enormous impact on the course of World War II. Synthetic oil can be produced from alternative fossil energy sources such as gas, coal, lignite and tar sands.[1] The Germans manufactured a limited amount of synthetic oil during World War II, and this procedure became popular later during the apartheid regime in South Africa. In the end, however, mass production was never realized.

In early 1941 Kopp travelled from Algeria to Vichy. It was the capital of unoccupied France, but in practice the difference was not so great. Marshal Pétain, hero of World War I and now fascist for the occasion, danced to the tune of the occupier. The regime, for example, was hardly reluctant to hand over Jews, French prisoners of war were held there and Vichy had to bear the cost of the occupation of the greater part of France itself.

In this fragmented France Kopp attempted to sell his expertise as an engineer. In May 1941 he moved to Marseille, where he lived at various addresses while establishing a laboratory to produce synthetic oil, adapted from the raw materials which were available: lignite (a kind of brown coal) was abundant in Bouches-du-Rhône. From 1st September 1941 until his departure 7th September 1943, he stayed at 48 Rue Boudouresque, situated close to the sea, from which he wrote his letter to George and Evelyn (as mentioned in the previous chapter). The street still exists today. He clearly struggled with the fact that he worked for the Vichy regime and thus potentially for the German fascists:

> *By then, I was offered by a French officer to remain here and do some really useful technical work which has actually, far more to do with fighting Germany and any war experience I have had before. The men who can do that sort of job are extremely few, and they sort of appealed to me not to let the beaten country down and I couldn't help staying. They gave me every possible guarantee that my work is not to serve anybody else but France and is helping to fight Germany. I have tried to establish contacts with official people abroad, with the Belgian Government in London too in order to get some sort of approbation or criticism of my doings and learn whether they want to go on or move or do something else. But I got no reply, remain a sort of free-lance which under present conditions, I rather hate to be.*[2]

Reading between the lines, he is trying to convince himself more than anyone else. Kopp was a smart man, but he perhaps underestimated the dangers of the Vichy regime. Either way, he had no alternative.

He goes on to state that a Lieutenant Onyett, whom he had met in captivity, was wounded in both arms and his left hand was missing. He hopes that someone will warn the British authorities and Onyett's wife – even if it is the person controlling and censoring his letters. Typical Kopp humour, though also illustrative of his helpful nature.

He assumes correctly that many of his British comrades have been called to arms. Orwell had enlisted with the Home Guard, an auxiliary army corps which in the event of an invasion was to defend Great Britain. Laurence O'Shaughnessy, his brother in law, had been killed during the evacuation of the British army in Dunkirk. He ends with the somewhat desperate thought that he hadn't seen his friends and girlfriends for almost two years: 'Give my love to Eileen and Eric, to Gwen and Eric, to little Laurence, to Doreen.'

On 1st June 1942 he finally succeeded in contacting MI5 with the help of Philippe Keun, a Dutchman who also fought in the Foreign Legion. Kopp claimed that he helped him to make maps. He let Keun use his office so that he could meet undisturbed with other agents who worked for the intelligence service of the French naval forces. Keun, who worked under the pseudonym Colonel Abel Dumas, was then taken over by MI5 with the approval of the French. In June Keun sent a letter to MI5, dated 29th May, with the request to have Kopp screened. In the short letter Keun states that Kopp was willing not only to put his expertise of synthetic oil at their disposal, but also a prototype of an anti-tank gun.

The next letter in Kopp's MI5 file is a long plea for himself. He repeats that he initially thought the best way he could fight the Germans was by helping the Vichy regime to manufacture synthetic oil, and he had built his semi-industrial laboratory for that purpose. But then things began to change:

If Germany should take drastic measures against France, they will probably be brutal and sudden, with Germany taking over the whole economic system of the country. An unobtrusive stoppage of my works would then be impossible, and even if I, personally, refused to carry on, my staff under German menace and control, could still operate them. However great is my wish to serve France, I cannot take the risk of having worked for the enemy.[3]

According to him he had started the laboratory with a capital of 500,000 francs lent by some friends and the Vichy government had promised him 100 million francs as a state participation.[4] However: 'Should the British authorities consider it highly probable that my work will become directly or indirectly useful to Germany I am prepared to bring it to an immediate end, and to take the necessary steps to indemnify my friends as soon as a transfer of funds is possible, between Belgium and Occupied France.'[5] This seems like a doubtful promise considering he left Belgium with considerable debts. He doesn't write it in so many words, but you can read between the lines that he hopes he will receive financial compensation from the British government. When Kopp was questioned in 1943 in Great Britain after the sudden shutdown of his espionage activities, he changed his version of events:

> Informant claims that he received no remuneration at all from the French Government [...]. He claims to have spent 600,000 francs on his scheme, adding that this came from his own pocket. [...] It may seem strange that informant who admitted that his financial status had suffered a loss at the time of his divorce in 1936, and the succeeding years being spent mainly in the Spanish army and French Foreign Legion, it is questionable how he had this large sum at his disposal. He was asked by examiner whether he had found a backer, but he again emphasized that it was his own money.[6]

It is likely that he never saw a penny. The demobilization report, moreover, bulges with contradictions, but this will be dealt with later.

The letter closes with an offer of his services to Great Britain. He encloses a CV with several references, among others from Orwell: 'In 1936, joined the Spanish regular Republican Army and remained in Spain until Dec. 1938. For details of this period, see Mr Eric Blair (address below) and his book "Homage to Catalonia".'[7] Quite interesting that he mentions a literary work as a recommendation. He understandably uses his knowledge of several languages as a trump: 'Speaks and writes French, English and Spanish; speaks and writes German and Dutch, understands Russian.'[8] The first reactions were positive:

> We have no unfavourable trace of the man on record, but he appears to be a very rough diamond [...], he would appear to be a suitable candidate as a S.O.E. agent.[9] [...] The only evidence

we have throwing light on this man's political sympathies consists in what is known of his contacts in the past. These include, in December 1938, the ILP in this country, and about the same time POUM in Spain: at that time 6328, as might be expected was in conflict with the orthodox Communist Party.[10] [...] From a letter written by 6328 from the South of France in December 1941 it appears that among his friends was Eric Blair @ George Orwell (the well-known political writer) who in 1937 was a volunteer with the ILP contingent of the International Brigade in Spain. From the above it appears that 6328 is a Marxist, but probably a Trotskyite and not a member of the Communist Party (We hardly think that Trotskyites can be considered as reliable as Stalinists in the present time). I should perhaps be added that Blair @ Orwell is known to have been in November 1941 a more whole-hearted supporter of the Allied War Effort than the Orthodox or Stalinite Communists.

This is followed by caution: '6328 is not to be employed for the moment, awaiting comments from HA and FA.'[11] The date is 9th June 1942. It is surprising how the civil servant prefers a Stalinist over a Trotskyite, explicable perhaps in light Stalin's war effort against Hitler. A second evaluation on 13th July is outright destructive:

Here is another offer to make synthetic petrol, with no details of the 'know how' [...]. I certainly will not fall for such a vague scheme. What is evident in this story is that KOPP has let himself in for certain financial commitments with friends who have fallen for his inventions, and now wants us to pay the piper for him and to guarantee his future expenditure on inventions for the practicability of which we have only his word. KOPP must be a rather naive individual.[12]

The author of the letter is rather suspicious about the fact that Kopp knew Abel Dumas, the French agent. The letter is typed but somebody has written: 'Telegram sent to Abel this day, saying matter of no interest.'

The file then falls silent for some months. In November 1942 a certain 'Sd'[13] Marcel Roost, a highly ranked civil servant of the Belgian intelligence service, reported in French on Kopp. We now know that he used Marc Jottard, the Belgian consul in Barcelona in 1938, as a source.[14] Jottard thought it likely that Kopp was a Belgian, writing that he was one of the few officers of the POUM to have been saved probably because he was a foreigner. Based on long conversations with Kopp, Jottard characterizes him as an intelligent and cultivated man, but considers him unsuitable 'for the current state of affairs as we see it'.[15] Strange, you would think such an intelligent and cultivated man would be considered an asset. Two valuable conclusions can be drawn from this statement: it is the first solid proof that Kopp had contact with the Belgian government, and it confirms the assumption that they had nothing to do with his release.

On 1st November 1942 Kopp writes that he has stopped the production of synthetic oil because of the high risk of the Germans wiping out the Vichy regime. He had secured a position as consulting engineer for a fuel company at Narbonne and was able to stay in Marseille because he only travelled to Narbonne once a week. In this way he found time to develop a network, using his job as a cover. Gradually his network grew in importance, and he contacted the British intelligence service one more time.

In March 1943 there is a sudden influx of documents in Kopp's MI5 file. A certain Olivier, an active spy in France, asks for information – Kopp clearly has been working for MI5 despite the earlier negative advice. Perhaps they made the best of a bargain and took over his network. Olivier, who was active under Kopp, sums up what he knows of him, which is not much: 'About 35 years old, height about 1m. 78, stoutish, fair hair closely clipped, prominent grey-blue eyes. Left thumb missing. He has only one lung. Speaks fluently English, German and Russian.'[16] But then the information becomes blurry. Olivier estimates him at thirty-five: Kopp was then forty-one. He had worked in the oil fields of Russia between 1928 and 1933: not true. He had been a general in the Spanish Republican Army: not true. He does know that Kopp is divorced, has five children and is Roman Catholic because 'he says grace before meals'. He concludes, 'On the whole, he is a very strange man, who seems to be very interested in money.'[17]

A new, slightly adapted CV with new references in also included in Kopp's file. This time they checked three references: P.H. Spaak, R.O. Stokes and G. Orwell. As mentioned before, P.H. Spaak, Belgian minister of foreign affairs, did not remember him. R.O. Stokes only testified in July, claiming that he had met Kopp in Ghent in 1931 for business. Kopp was then an engineer mechanic and metallurgist. Kopp was employed by the Centrales Electriques des Flandres et du Brabant in Langerbrugge, situated in the Ghent Canal Zone. This explains his knowledge of Dutch as Ghent is a Flemish town. They continued corresponding, but didn't hear from him for some time after 1934, until he suddenly presented himself in his London office shortly after the end of the Spanish Civil War. Kopp did stay in London during that period:

> Kopp informed Stokes that he had lost his wife and had been left with his five children to care for, but that he had managed to get them fostered and had then joined the Spanish Republican Army in Spain. He was promoted to a Brigadier, and at the close of hostilities had made his way to his country. Mr Stokes said that he had not seen or heard of KOPP since, but understood that it was his intention to go to Paris, as he could not return to Belgium as he was an anti-Rexist.[18] Mr Stokes stated that, although that he had not known KOPP intimately enough to judge him wholly, he regarded him as very anti-Nazi, courageous, loyal and absolutely trustworthy.[19]

Kopp did go to Paris, but he was allowed to enter Belgium by the authorities – even though he was anti-fascist and thus anti-Rexist.[20]

The third reference of July 1943 is that of Orwell – a most interesting letter for MI5 it seems, as under the letterhead is scribbled: 'many thanks this is most helpful'.[21] Orwell testifies that he became acquainted with Kopp in 1937 when serving in the 29th Division of the POUM. Then Orwell says that Kopp was later transferred to the 128th Division. This means that Orwell did know that Kopp had made a switch, which he does not mention in *Homage to Catalonia*, but his information is rather hazy. When he mentions the 128th Division he probably means the 128th Brigade and he does not mention Kopp's important change to the 45th Brigade of the Army of the East.[22] 'In about June 1937 KOPP was arrested as a Trotskyite and detained in prison without trial for about a year. On release he came to this country and stayed for two or three months with BLAIR's parents at Greenwich.' This seems bizarre. Perhaps he did not want to incriminate Gwen, the widow of Laurence, whom Kopp stayed with in reality. Then he repeats Kopp's old story: '[He] had to leave Belgium because he was sympathetic to the Spanish democratic cause, and at the factory where he was working, had surreptitiously made armaments for Spain. He was warned about his conduct and got away to Paris. He could not return while he was on the Belgian Army Reserve.' It is clear that Orwell still believed this. On the other hand he did see, be it partly, through his friend: 'He regarded Kopp as a loyal man, possessed of anti-Nazi sentiments, but otherwise not deeply interested in politics although mildly Left Wing. He was physically courageous and resolute and, generally speaking, an adventurer. He had a tendency, however, to embellish things, and although deserving of confidence in his personal conduct, one hesitated to accept anything he said without additional corroboration.'[23] Govaerts finds it very unlikely that Orwell, a merciless observer, would have fallen for Kopp's lies.[24] Although he did not actually discover the complete truth, he did realize that Kopp was not always trustworthy.

We know that Captain Courtenay Fox collected these three testimonials on the orders of one Major Anthony Blunt. The Blunt case is a story on its own. The KGB recruited him in 1934, and it was he who convinced the famous trio Kim Philby, Guy Burgess and Donald Maclean – better known as the Cambridge Spies – to work for the Soviets. During the war Blunt passed decoded German messages on to the Russians. He was a well-known art historian, specialized in French art and was appointed keeper of the Queen's paintings. He received a knighthood in 1956. In 1964 MI5 found out that he was a double spy, but it took until 1979 for him to be finally unmasked by Prime Minister Thatcher. He fell into disgrace and died three years later. In this respect it is rather ironic that Blunt had Kopp screened: Blunt had control over whether candidate spies were to be trusted, while he himself was not.

Chapter 9

SPY... OR DOUBLE SPY?

In the summer of 1943 Germany licked its wounds after the Battle of Stalingrad. The Allied forces prepared themselves in the West for D-Day and had already landed in Sicily. In Vichy France there were no signs of the Germans weakening. Quite the contrary, the German stranglehold which had made Kopp cease his quest for synthetic oil worsened. He refers to this situation in a letter sent to Orwell and Eileen on 26th July 1943. It is clear he had been working for MI5 for some time at this point:

When you last heard of me, my work with the French Government was about to be interrupted owing to increased German control, and I was attempting to make contacts with the British to be allowed to sort of still be doing at least something in this war. [...][1]

Well, for about a year now, these contacts have been achieved and I am working hard. I consider it a privilege to go on 'fighting' although my wounds have prevented me from taking any active part in any regular sort of service. I am feeling quite happy and glorious. Besides I have retained a sort of Consulting Engineer post with the Ministry of Industrial Production, it is not a full time job and does not prevent me from performing my other duties; far from it.

He does not complain explicitly, but admits that bouts of malaria bother him and that food is scarce. He refers to his house on Rue Boudouresque, Marseille: 'I am still living in the same place near the sea, with a coastal battery manned by Germans 300 feet away; I am often speculating upon the accuracy of up-to-date bombing; according to pre-war averages, they would be sure, aiming at the battery, to knock my place down.'

Kopp supposes they know that his mother had passed away in September 1942, adding that the children are well.[2] He expects that his oldest son, Michel, who is already taller than him, will soon be able to help him with all the activities of the resistance.

Then follows an interesting passage in which we catch a glimpse of his political and military insight. On the same day that he wrote the letter he had learned that Mussolini had been deposed. He predicts that:

> *Italy will collapse soon and I expect it might have an influence upon the duration of the war, although I remain rather pessimistic as for the lenght [sic] of German resistance; people reckon it in months or even weeks, but I persist to think the bastards will fight desperately for another couple of years; this is a political sort of war and everybody in Germany who is holding any sort of post, from dictator to postman, knows he will loose [sic] it when Germany capitulates and the régime changes; it is something akin to what happened in republican Spain; they will all refrain as long as they can from avowing they are beaten.*[3]

Prophetic words. He ends his letter with greetings to Doreen, Gwen and to the Masons.[4]

Again we must fall back on the demobilization report to reconstruct the following months. Its veracity is not outstanding and it bulges with contradictions. Kopp was then back in Great Britain and clearly the sole source upon which the interviewer relied. He even writes, 'In accordance with instructions received, informant's [Kopp] organization was not investigated thoroughly by the undersigned [Harper], who, however, following instructions, took full details of the man's life history.'[5] Perhaps this version of his CV was checked on its reliability later, but no traces can be found of this in his file.

The document consists of five pages and covers the life of our protagonist. It makes a promising start, listing all the pseudonyms which he has used during his French period: 'Georges alias Georges Henri Dubreuil, alias Georges Kerbras, alias Georges Henry.'[6] But then it begins: of course, Kopp calls himself a Belgian. His mother 'Henriette Neman' was born in the Flemish town 'Maesyck' (now Maaseik). Subsequently we hear of his school career and fictitious military service, followed by his professional career before he went to war. His adventures in Spain are puffed up with his invention of the apocryphal anti-tank device, supposedly the reason for his arrest: 'When reaching BARCELONA to take over his command about the end of June or beginning of July, 1937, informant was arrested by the Guepeou who wanted to obtain full particulars about his invention for RUSSIA. Informant refused to disclose anything, simply, he states, on account of the way he had been treated.'[7] The audacity of Kopp to keep spinning these yarns is remarkable. Later it will become clear that he was not only an inventor of stories, but also a real inventor. We can presume, though, that he ever actually had the concept of an anti-tank device in his head, and the fact remains that no material traces of such a weapon have been found.

After the Spanish period Kopp mentions the interlude in Great Britain, followed by his activities in the Foreign Legion and in occupied France. He was particularly active in espionage and the resistance during the period of November 1942 to September 1943. First for the Deuxième Bureau and the French admiralty of the Vichy regime, and from March 1943, when the German influence strengthened, for the French resistance in service of MI5 and the British admiralty. The key question is whether he worked for both sides and subsequently was a double spy. Professor Davison suggests this in his book *The Lost Orwell*, though he does not have any hard evidence. It is doubtful that Kopp willingly worked for both sides and was playing them off against each other: the step from the French to the British was logical because of the growing German factor, and even if he had worked for both sides it would be excusable. Who does not make one's hands dirty in a war? More incriminating is the fact that his collaborators had the impression that he was keen on money. And lest it be forgotten, Kopp was an inventor – he created things all through his life. If it wasn't synthetic oil, it was a supposed anti-tank gun or some other device. The love of creation made him do weird things.

Towards the end of 1942, when he traded in the Deuxième Bureau for MI5, Kopp had probably been in Belgium. Anne-Marie Kopp was then in secondary education in Uccle. The principal came to fetch her saying that her 'papa' was waiting for her in the playground. Anne-Marie was worried because she did not believe that it could be her father, and if it was her grandfather Warnotte, then something had to have happened. Downstairs Georges Kopp was effectively waiting with the whole family. He had audaciously enquired in the city hall where his children were. A daring and shrewd venture, as the Germans had control over the administration. Some time later as they walked on the street, they happened to meet their mother. Kopp was dressed conspicuously in a *pied-de-poule* jacket with jodhpurs and boots. Anne-Marie thought that he used the fancy clothing as a smokescreen. Only a collaborator would show off his wealth in this way; one would never expect an undercover agent to dress like that. She does not remember how he had got there, though her brother Jean always asserted that he was dropped into Belgium with a parachute. If this was a boyish fantasy, we may never know as Jean died some time ago.

The demobilization report does not mention much about Kopp's spying activities, nor do any of the other available written sources. According to Quentin Kopp he was named after one of his father's fellow spies. Quentin's mother Doreen Hunton believed that it was on the basis of Georges's information that the Brits bombed the harbour of Brest.[8, 9] A particularly striking story was that her husband owed his life to a wallet which he always wore near his heart region and which apparently stopped a German bullet.

The report does mention that Michel Kopp, the eldest son, and his father could have worked together. Michel Kopp denies it:

My father came from England to the Continent in 1941 and in 1942 and probably on other occasions as a liaison agent of MI5 with the French and the Belgian underground organizations. I have no information on those particular contacts. Being born in 1926 I was 15 or 16 years old in those days. My father met me twice and the last time put me in touch with people who could help me [escape from] *Belgium via France and Spain and eventually in England in October 1943 when I enlisted in the Belgian Army (just a Brigade at the time integrated into the British Army). Incidentally, in order to be eligible for enrolment I had to pretend to be born in 1925 and therefore 18 years old instead of 17.[10]*

At one point of time my father may have thought I might be able to help him, but when he met me in 1942 it must have been obvious to him that I was too young for espionage or that kind of work in occupied Belgium. My joining the Belgian Brigade at the end of 1943 had nothing to do with my father except that he tipped me on the right channels to use to get to England. Once over there I didn't have any contact with him. My military service at the time and until the end of the war when I was in OCTU [Officer Cadet Training Unit] *was purely Army and not under cloak business.*[11]

This begs the question: how can this be when even Anthony Blunt believed that Georges's son had been working for MI5? The MI5 file remains a source of wonder.

Georges Kopp himself claimed that he sometimes operated behind the enemy lines and therefore had to cling 'as Ulysses' to the bottom of train carriages. Some sentences in the report refer to the obtaining of intelligence on the German defence lines on the coast, for which Kopp was assisted by French customs officers. When they did not collect enough data he appealed to André Jouve, a law student, who he found via a liaison agent, Julien Paul, alias Polo. Jouve had been conscripted for obligatory labour in Germany. Because his uncle was town clerk he provided him with false identity papers in which he was recorded as eighteen years old, meaning he was too young and could evade a summons. Kopp thought he was a decent chap and drafted him on 1st August 1943. Since Jouve had no experience whatsoever, Kopp took care of him. Because of that the boy knew where he lived and had knowledge of Kopp's identity.

On 26th August the Gestapo caught Jouve red-handed near Cap Pinède in Marseille. Despite Kopp's warnings he had a plan of the local defence systems and batteries in his coat pocket. Luckily Polo shadowed the boy during his first missions and he managed to warn the others. Kopp instructed everyone in the organization to lie low and reported to London via radio. Two days later Kopp left for Paris, where he met his chief 'Fitzroy' and delivered his report. On 3rd September he wrote a letter to Polo, instructing him to join him in Paris on 7th September, but Polo did not show up. Fitzroy then gave him the order to flee to Great Britain.

Thus Kopp's adventure in France ended. Whether or not the Gestapo succeeded in rounding up the organization and how Kopp fled isn't recorded anywhere. What is certain is that he stayed in London shortly after his flight, since the first entry of his Aliens Order Registration Certificate is on 15th September 1943.[12]

MI5 probably evacuated Kopp with a Lysander from France[13]

Quentin Kopp knows for sure that after the collapse of the espionage network his father was evacuated in 1943 in a Westland Lysander III, a single-engine airplane that you can still find in the War Museum at Duxford in Cambridgeshire. This is quite likely because the Brits typically used the Lysander for sea rescues and other difficult circumstances.

Kopp had no Belgian nationality and never served in the Belgian army, and his previous residence was Gibraltar. Perhaps he was brought via Gibraltar, which is British territory, to Great Britain.

Chapter 10

GENTLEMAN, FARMER, INVENTOR

After his demobilization Kopp temporarily moved in with Gwen O'Shaughnessy, who still lived at 24 Crooms Hill, near the Royal Observatory in Greenwich. There he met Doreen Hunton (Gwen's half sister), Orwell, Eileen and his friends in the ILP. Eight months of civil war and eighteen months of excruciating prison regime in Spain, ten months of nomadic existence in London and Paris, sixteen months in the French Foreign Legion and finally thirty months as a spy for the Vichy regime and MI5 had taken their toll. If his spirit was not broken, his body was.

After his arrival in Great Britain, Kopp tried to settle down. This proved difficult to begin with. He had not managed to acquire very much money from MI5 in exchange for his expertise in the field of synthetic oil. Worse, MI5 doubted his integrity again, and things did not improve when the service received the testimony of a certain Mr Lance. Lance worked in the War Room of the Ministry of Home Security and happened to meet Kopp. Lance thought he was a Belgian and knew he had recently been to France. He had fought with Kopp in the International Brigades in Spain 'and had seen enough of him to form the opinion that he was a doubtful character and the type of man who was prepared to do any sort of work for the highest bidder'.[1] Lance, then, felt it his duty to warn those concerned of Kopp's presence in the country: 'For all he knew Kopp might be here with the highest motives. On the other hand he might be up to no good.'[2] Kopp had given him his address: 19 Vincent Square, and the telephone number: VIC, 2633.[3]

It is a puzzling testimony. Lance placed Kopp in the International Brigades. This means that they must have met just before his arrest in Spain because before this he had served in the POUM. Or Lance did not want to admit that he had been a Poumista. He did not give any particular arguments as to why he thought Kopp was not to be

24 Crooms Hill, Greenwich. This was Gwen O'Shaughnessy and her
husband Eric's home. Eric was Eileen O'Shaughnessy's brother and was
killed at Dunkirk. He was a very distinguished heart surgeon who pioneered
many operations. It was the family's central point and the home where
Georges Kopp and Doreen Hunton met.

trusted, and the MI5 file does not contain any measures which prove
that they took Lance's allegation seriously. On the contrary, they tried
to help Kopp to build a new life in the ensuing months. In short, one
cannot draw any significant conclusions from this, except for the fact
that he did not stay with Gwen.

After that Kopp's MI5 file slowly runs dry. From January 1944
until the last letter of 2nd June 1944, Blunt and his aide Courtenay
Young occupied themselves getting his work permit in order and did
their utmost to get him employed as a technical assistant with the firm
R.O. Stokes & Co. Ltd., 538/540 Salisbury House in London. The
firm worked for the Ministry of Supply and was specialized in non-
ferrous development control. This is the same R.O. Stokes whom
he knew from Belgium and one of the references in his CV. Stokes
wanted to take him, but Kopp was an 'alien' and therefore a lot of

hurdles had to be cleared. Blunt thought that Great Britain owed him that because:

(a) **KOPP** has personally rendered very considerable services in our organization, (b) **KOPP**'s son is still working for us at a not inconsiderable risk to himself, (c) if **KOPP** takes his present position which we have found for him we shall not only have satisfied our moral obligations which were clearly to find him a position where he could earn a reasonable living with work congenial to him, but also we shall in point of fact be establishing him in a situation where he will subsequently get foreign contacts enabling him to travel abroad and be of further use to us.[4]

Blunt seems to still have great plans for him, but to our knowledge nothing came from it. An entry in Kopp's Aliens Order Registration Certificate confirms that Kopp, at least temporarily, accepted the post with Stokes.

The last fact worth mentioning is in a letter of 7th March 1944, addressed to Blunt. A marriage is planned for 11th March, and for this Kopp urgently needs a certificate. There is no mention of the name Doreen Hunton, his future wife.

On 5th February Kopp had already moved to Canonbury Square, Islington in London. In October George Orwell and Eileen also rented a flat there. In June they had adopted a boy named Richard, and Doreen and Georges regularly babysat for the little one while Orwell was working on the Continent as a war correspondent following the invading Allied troops.[5] On 24th February 1945 Doreen had her first baby, Stephen. He would later die in 1964 of a kidney disease after one of the pioneering transplant operations at St Mary's Hospital, Paddington.

Eileen, much like Orwell, showed a surprising contempt for health, and paid the price for it. In the beginning of March 1945 she became seriously ill, but concealed it from her husband, who left for Cologne to follow the Allied troops. Even most of her friends were not aware that she was gravely ill. Eileen was diagnosed with tumours in her uterus and had to undergo a hysterectomy, but had postponed it because she felt a 'hysterical' longing to give Orwell a child, and later because a possible cancer would have prevented the adoption of Richard.[6] She went to the Fernwood House Hospital in Newcastle for the operation because it was cheaper there: 'I really don't think I'm worth the money', she wrote, befitting her black humour.[7] Georges Kopp accompanied the toddler Richard and Eileen to King's Cross station and was subsequently the last of her friends to see her before her death. She wrote her final letter to George Orwell just before undergoing the operation: 'Dearest, I am just going to have an operation, already enema'd, injected with morphia in the right arm, (which is a nuisance), cleaned and packed up like a precious image in cotton wool and bandages. When it's over I'll add a note to this and it can get off quickly.'[8] She died during the operation on 29th March, immediately after anaesthesia had been administered. Five months later Orwell broke through with his publication of *Animal Farm*.

Eileen had hoped that the Kopps would raise Richard, but Orwell merely saw it as a temporary arrangement, because he did not want to educate his son in town. Perhaps the gradual cooling of their relationship played a role. Had Orwell been jealous of Kopp's relation with Eileen? It does not seem likely. Kopp's chronic lack of money may have been disruptive, but Orwell was quite generous. An ideological explanation could be plausible: Kopp, who was not a tremendous ideologist, evolved to the right wing of the political spectrum. Michel remembers a self-explanatory (though not very original) saying of his father: 'I would doubt a man's heart if he is not a socialist at the age of 20, but I would question his brains if he is not a liberal at 35!'[9] He moved, as so many ageing people do, from the Left to the Centre.

You could call him a pragmatist or at worst an opportunist. It goes without saying that Orwell also changed ideologically, but he remained a man of the Left who was convinced that capitalism led to greater tyranny than state interference. Consequently he was more inclined to be a political puritan. Or perhaps Orwell had idealized Kopp too much during his Spanish period. Didn't he once describe him as a heroic 'commandante' on a black horse? Then it is quite normal for Kopp to fall from his pedestal. There was no definitive fight, they just slid away from each other.

Toftcombs House

In 1945 Doreen and Kopp were able to buy Toftcombs House, a manor house with accompanying grounds near the Scottish town of Biggar, situated about thirty miles south-west and south-east respectively of Edinburgh and Glasgow. According to Michel Kopp they used his demobilization premium and Doreen's savings to pay for it. One glimpse of the map suffices to imagine the idyllic surroundings. Toftcombs House, surrounded by green, met all the standards of a typical Scottish manor house: more a little castle than a house, a bit gloomy, the reddish walls overgrown with ivy and with battlement-shaped gables. It must have been quite a premium, but according to Mary, Kopp's third child from the second marriage, Doreen came from a wealthy family and received a substantial inheritance.[10]

On 19th December 1945 they moved into their new house together with little Stephen. Georges contacted his eldest son Michel again and suggested that he stay with them. In this way he was able to start his higher studies in Edinburgh. In the mean time Michel had, as mentioned earlier, finished his military training with the unit of the British army from which the Brigade Piron originated.

Doreen, Georges and Quentin at Toftcombs House[11]

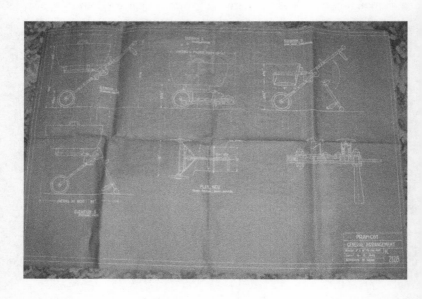

He took rooms in Edinburgh and stayed during many weekends in and around Toftcombs House. Living on the estate with his new wife Doreen and his children Michel, Stephen and Quentin (born 11th May 1947) must have given Kopp some much-needed rest. A photograph from this period seems to confirm this: Doreen holds the toddler Quentin upright on one of the two goats; Georges is feeding the animals; he sucks on his pipe, the sign of happiness in times long gone, and wears a leather jacket. It is symbolic of his gentleman-farmer period.

In a letter to his daughter of 13th February 1946 he writes in French of his life in Biggar: 'My life is that of an engineer in a small factory where one makes agricultural machines. It is a small business (forty employees), but it is very lively and very interesting. I still have time to occupy myself with my garden and nursery and to hunt [...]. I started a small nursery of poultry in a small meadow adjacent to the garden, and we shall have bees and a couple of goats; a pig too, for the coming Christmas party.'[12]

He never could sit still. Michel remembers that his father once demonstrated a sand-sieving machine which he had designed himself: 'He told me that he was discussing developing it full scale with a Scottish city for cleaning their beach. Apparently this project never materialised.'[13] This was probably because the time was not ripe for such an idea and because of the postwar shortages of funds. He really was ahead of his time and that has been the case with all his inventions. In those years he was constantly looking for that one creation which would save him financially. Illustrative of this is his 1949 plan for a 'pramcot', a pram which can be built to a buggy – a stunningly modern design.[14] In December 1949 he wrote to J. Oostwoud of the Oostwoud Factories, 20 Maliesingel, Utrecht about 'a transformable baby carriage which is particularly suited to people living in flats [...]. My own baby has one and seems quite happy in it, and my wife is delighted to push little Mary in her pramcot.'[15] He wanted Oostwoud to manufacture the buggy, but it never came about.

Chapter 11

TO BE OR NOT TO BE O'BRIEN

On 20th March Kopp wrote a letter to Orwell to invite him to Biggar: 'With rabbit shooting (legal now) and any amount of poaching, inclusive trout and salmon in the Tweed.' And he adds: 'You can have a jeep whenever you like.'[1] Orwell was renting a country house on Jura, one of the southernmost isles of the Hebrides, to be able to write without disturbance. A car would be useful for transporting supplies from Craighouse, Jura's port, to Barnhill.

In May 1946 Orwell spent a week in Toftcombs House. Before he left, Kopp again offered to sell Orwell an old Ford truck, which he could collect at the beginning of June. After some delay Orwell was able to collect it in Glasgow. When he tried to drive off the ferry in Craighouse, the vehicle did not move an inch. It had to be lifted from the ship with a crane. The engine had run out of cooling water and was a total loss. Orwell was furious and left the wreck behind on the quay, where it remained until 1976. Kopp, who as an engineer must have known that the Ford was in a poor condition, still had sold the car to his friend.

Despite this, their friendship survived. Orwell later bought a goose from Georges for the Christmas of 1946. In April 1947 Orwell told Gwen, his sister-in-law, that he had received a note in which Kopp announced the imminent birth of a baby, but he hadn't heard anything else since then. Quentin was born on 11th May 1947.

After that there must have been some contact, as Orwell invited Michel Kopp, Georges's eldest son, to stay in Barnhill during the summer of 1947:

My father rightly thought that to meet a man like Orwell would be a great experience for me. At the time Orwell and his sister lived in a house called Barnhill on the isle of Jura [...]. It was quite a trip to get there by train, car and ship. I believe I was bringing him a goose, but whether this was some sort of peace offering or just an ordinary present I don't remember.

I spent a week as a guest in Barnhill. It was a rather dilapidated farm house lent to Orwell by the local Lord (or Laird as they say in Scotland), a friend of Etonian days. His maiden sister was keeping house for him. She was a poor cook [...].

At the time Orwell was writing the book later published as '1984' [...]. Unfortunately I saw very little of the great man: he was working day and night at his book with perhaps the premonition it would be the last one and that death was lurking in the background. I used to see him mainly at supper time. He was looking in poor health, eating little, chain smoking and drinking a lot of coffee. His conversation was most fascinating although some parts of it dealing with political and philosophical topics passed over my head. Today I wish I could remember them.[2]

This testimony is completely in line with Orwell's image in his numerous biographies: everything had to give way for his writing, including his health, but when he felt like it (e.g., during supper) he loved to converse with friends, certainly about politics. In 1947 Orwell was in the midst of his masterwork *Nineteen Eighty-Four*, which was published in 1948. What student is not familiar with this work and its denouncement of the power of the media, the violation of privacy and the dangers of forging history? The omnipresent and yet invisible Big Brother leads the totalitarian power of Oceania. He crushes the protagonist Winston Smith and his beloved Julia because they resist the Party's directives.

One of the collaborators of Big Brother is the double spy O'Brien. He is a supposed member of the resistance, but in reality he works for the regime. O'Brien tortures Smith and brainwashes him until he loves his Leader. The book is a clear satire on communism under Stalin and the above-mentioned show trials.

Let us read a passage in which Orwell describes O'Brien: 'Winston was struck, as he had been struck before, by the tiredness of O'Brien's face. It was strong and fleshy and brutal, it was full of intelligence and a sort of controlled passion before which he felt himself helpless; but it was tired. There were pouches under the eyes; the skin sagged from the cheekbones.'[3] Doesn't O'Brien remind you of Kopp?

Another passage: 'He opened his eyes and looked up gratefully at O'Brien. At sight of the heavy, lined face, so ugly and so intelligent, his heart seemed to turn over. If he could have moved he would have stretched out a hand and laid it on O'Brien's arm. He had never loved him so deeply as at this moment, and not merely because he had stopped the pain. [...] In some sense that went deeper than friendship, they were intimates.'[4]

Jeffrey Meyers and later Gordon Bowker have both argued that Orwell was inspired by Kopp when he created the diabolical character O'Brien. Peter Davison is sceptical about this because he believes Orwell would not have betrayed their friendship like that. Of course the character in the novel and his friend are not identical, but psychologically it is plausible that he used Kopp as a source of inspiration. An author happens to pick bits and pieces from his life to create characters. Coincidence only explains so much, and O'Brien takes after Kopp a little too much: the fleshy face, the extreme tiredness, the intelligence, the fact that he was a double spy, and the love–hate relationship. It seems clear to me that Orwell had parts of Kopp's personality in mind when he created O'Brien.

And there is more. Winston Smith stands, as the common name suggests, as a symbol for the everyman. Still, no one doubts that the creation of Smith was based on Orwell himself – it is commonly known that Orwell was terrified of rats. To bring Winston Smith to his knees, he has to lose all respect for himself. O'Brien achieves this by forcing him to betray his beloved Julia. O'Brien sees through his victim and confronts him with his worst fears in Room 101. For Winston this is the fear of rats. He is buckled into a chair and O'Brien places a kind of fencing mask on his head. Behind that there is a cage with colossal, famished rats. A small gate separates the rats from the mask. If O'Brien opens the gate they will jump into the mask and wolf themselves on Winston's head. Winston wants to give his life for his love but cannot resist his phobia of rats, and he saves himself by betraying Julia. Thus he loses all the values he fought for and becomes a zombie.

In Orwell's *Homage to Catalonia* the rats are a recurrent theme. For example: '"There are rats, rats, / Rats as big as cats, / In the quartermaster's store!"'[5] The ones at La Granja itself really were as big as cats, or nearly; great bloated brutes that waddled over the beds of muck, too impudent even to run away unless you shot at them.'[6] 'And the rats which were a public nuisance and would even devour leather belts and cartridge-pouches.'[7] 'The filthy brutes came swarming out of the ground on every side. If there is one thing I hate more than another it is a rat running over me in the darkness.'[8]

Whether Kopp was afraid of rats is not generally known. The fact is that, just like Orwell, he was confronted with them daily and that, by sharing his experiences in prison with him, he unknowingly strengthened Orwell's phobia. That Kopp was brutally cross-examined in Spain by the Russian secret police was mentioned before. An article from *L'Espagne Nouvelle* of 15th January, probably based on Kopp's testimony, states the following: 'He was thrown for 12 consecutive days in a filthy cell, full of rats, without food and without drinkable water and during those days he only heard one thing: "Tonight we are going to shoot you".'

It is odd to think how rats and torture connect Kopp and Orwell. To create the character O'Brien, Orwell more than likely picked out some of his friend's characteristics. Not so much to hurt him, more to create a round character: an author can have no scruples in the creation of a masterpiece.

Kopp may have read *Nineteen Eighty-Four*, as the book was published in 1948, some time before his death. He will have recognized himself in O'Brien and will have smiled, full of admiration for Orwell's genius. Just as his perfidious counterpart O'Brien, he was full of contradictions. Truth is a lie. A lie is truth.

On 21st January 1950 George Orwell died from complications resulting from tuberculosis. Did Kopp have the chance to visit him in the sanatorium near Glasgow? Did he assist at the burial in Sutton Courtenay? Did he ever stand before Orwell's grave at the All Saints' Churchyard and read the simple epitaph: 'Here lies Eric Arthur Blair, born June 25th 1903, died January 21st 1950'? It is possible because Kopp only worked from 11th March 1950 on in France. The name Kopp appears in Orwell's will, regarding an outstanding debt of £250. That made him the biggest debtor of Sonia Brownwell, the young wife whom Orwell married on his deathbed and who was consequently his biggest heir. She acquitted his debt.

Chapter 12

DOWNHILL

In the idyllic Toftcombs House laid the origins of Kopp's downfall. It is likely that the mortgage and the costs to maintain the estate were a heavy burden on the family. Moreover he had to keep two babies and a student. The letters to Anne-Marie show that he worked hard to make something of his life. In 1947 he wrote from a London club that he had to travel a lot. During his previous train journey it had been too hot in his compartment: 'He had taken care of two young ladies. One of four and one of sixteen months who had sat on his knee, while mum was resting in the corridor.'[1] According to Anne-Marie that was typical for her father: if he saw a young woman, he worked himself to the bone to please her. In 1948 his second son Pierre came to stay with him. Georges found a job for him on a Welsh farm, but after a year he returned to Belgium. His father would later find him a job on a farm in Normandy.

Kopp's health was gradually deteriorating. On 11th July 1947 he wrote to his daughter:

It is obvious that my four injuries which followed on a period of big concerns in terms of feelings, the years of clandestine work, and finally my two 'phlebitis' haven't been there without causing big damage. I will never accept that I am an invalid, a mister of pills which have to provide for health. I will continue to lead an active life and to flog my organism and obtain the service of it that I want. I still can, with a right leg which was pierced on seventeen places, walk 50 km a day or go hunting in the hills for a whole afternoon; I can still work 16 hours a day and build ingenious machines which really work, I can spend nights without sleeping in crowded trains and sit 12 hours at the wheel; women still find me interesting.[2]

Kopp needed a lot of money, but he was no businessman and to make matters worse his inventions did not particularly catch on.[3] He must have come close to success, however, with his 'Tinto Heater': an economical heater which worked on petrol.[4] Some of his designs include a Tinto oil control, oil tank, control valves, burner connection and a spark plug. Indeed, two thirds of his business correspondence relates to the Tinto Heater, which proves that it was his showpiece.[5] It begins on 1st September 1947; he reports to a certain Mr Schmitt that he is testing a heater – not yet called the Tinto Heater or Burner. In the years that followed his project seemed to run well. He designed a series of prototypes. A few firms seemed to be interested and he kept on applying for patents in Europe, America and Canada. He worked with a civil engineer, the Dane Ivar Thomsen, who mediated with companies to take the Tinto in production.[6]

The correspondence is generally business-like, but here and there something can be learned of Kopp's private life. A letter of 4th July 1949 to the firm Hansen and Cox, with establishments in Denmark and Canada, teaches us that Kopp wasn't able to go abroad because of an accident. Whether this is true remains the question. It was not at all easy for him to travel abroad as an 'alien'. He did invite a representative of Hansen and Cox, a certain Mr Lewin from the Avenue des Renardeaux in Ghent, for a stay in London. Kopp mentions the club where he will lodge: Farmers' Club, 3 Whitehall Court. On 19th July he reports to Thomson, the intermediary. Lewin had accepted the invitation: 'I have the impression that Mr Lewin's object was mainly exploration, that he made a reconnaissance to establish what kind of fish I am. In any case he did not conceal that he was "entirely sold on Tinto", to use his own slang, which in King's English means that he is convinced that Tinto is a good proposition.'[7]

According to his children Kopp could spend money as no other. He lived from day to day and stayed unrealistically optimistic. All these factors together – mortgage, maintenance of the estate and family, moderate health, moderate business mind – led inevitably to financial problems. In 1948 they had to sell their estate and on 26th August the family moved to Shallcross Manor in Whaley Bridge, in the middle of the rural Peak District, 'to be closer to my

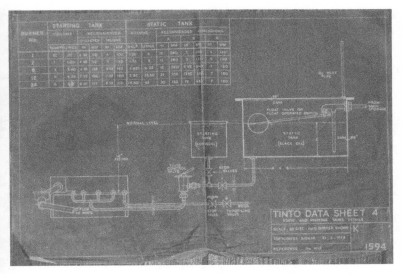

One of the numerous designs of parts of his Tinto Heater[8]

clients'.[9] Michel, who wanted to continue his studies in Edinburgh, was awarded a scholarship and did some odd jobs to make ends meet. On 30th January Doreen and Georges's last child, Mary, was born. The agricultural machines business went on the rocks, according to his children because his business partner had deceived him.[10] In February 1949 the last servant of the household was dismissed.

On September 1949 the Danish company Recks Opvarmnings Comp. Kedel og Maskinfabrikanter announced that, if everything went well, it would bring the Tinto Burners onto the market. On 24th October the Kopp family moved to 2 Wells Street, Rugby.

From February 1950 onwards the business correspondence contained negative messages. He negotiated via Thomsen with the firm N.G.K. Tholand, Esq. in New York to bring his Tinto in production there. In a second letter he had already asked for 5,000 dollars. The financial need of Kopp must have been huge:

My wife's health has been deteriorating lately and she is advised to go for a few months to the South of France, starting as soon as possible. She has had

Shallcross Manor

a very hard war, night ambulance driving all through the London blitz +
full time clerical war job, this being followed by 3 children in 4 years, not to
speak of the strain of having to live with a husband like me.[11] These 3 small
children would have to go with her, which implies a journey by car. Mine
(10 years old) died on me some time ago, and the delivery of a new car in
this country takes now at least 3 years.

  I had planned to solve this difficulty thanks to the 5000 dollars which I
am expecting from you. We can get delivery of a new car off the shelf under
a personal export scheme if we pay for it in hard currency.

A strange story, especially when one bears in mind that he would leave
for France on 11th March 1950 in the hope that he could appeal to
his old network of friends and relations again.

   In France it went from bad to worse. In a registered letter of
4th April – addressed to George Kopp, Esq., in Hotel Tatin, La
Motte Beuvron, Loir et Cher – a patent officer, A.C. Ashton, declares
that Tholand does not want to give 5,000 dollars to them, and what
is worse Kopp still owes the fees for filing fifteen patent applications
on the American continent. There is also a letter which mentions 4,

Kopp's permit for temporary residence in France

Boulevard Raspail Paris, 7ième as his address, so he was on the move constantly. Anne-Marie and Michel Kopp met him in Paris in 1950.

The documents of 14th September 1950 seem to indicate a turn of events. A notary named Mallier sent to Kopp's address (this time 2 Avenue Hoche in Paris) a copy of the purchase deed to the Brennes estate, a property situated in the hamlets Isdes and Vilemurlin, in the region of the Loire, close to Orléans. The sellers were two sisters and a brother of the Landron family in Meung-sur-Loire. The description of the domain appeals to the imagination: it is an estate with a central building, a forester's house, two farms, a coach house, lakes, meadows and forests. In the accompanying letter the notary admonishes Kopp to bring his paper work in order; since Kopp had the status of non-residing alien in France, he had to meet strict conditions.

In the meantime Kopp had ceased relations with Recks Opvarmnings Comp. Kedel- og Maskinfabrikanter, but he had several contacts with the Danish firm Olesen & Fetterlein. Things did not improve there either and Kopp terminated the collaboration with the intermediary Ivar Thomsen. On 12th January 1951 Kopp received a conciliatory letter from the firm: a certain Mr Rassow was the new intermediary and he was supposed to remove all the misunderstandings concerning the Tinto Burner.

Then in a handwritten letter of 20th March 1951, Kopp complains that the Danes have not kept their promises, and owe him among other things 1,100,000 French francs.[12] Because of this he cannot not fulfil his obligations towards the Landron family, the sellers of the Brennes estate, and he is in a complete mess. The tone of the letter is desperate: 'It seems to me that I shall never get disentangled from difficulties created by people who do not keep their word. I cannot work and make money when I have no money to start with, no home, no food, no clothes, and no tools.'[13] Only on the second page does it become clear that the letter is addressed to his wife Doreen: 'I am sure, Doreen, that you will bring up our children in the best possible way, and that you will have the strength of mind and body to do this against reasonable odds, which restarting without me, without my tangle of commitments, would leave you to face.' He ends with a gloomy overview of his professional career: 'I have given all I had. [...] Most of the work I have done these last years has been bought by people who did not pay for it, and left me in the lurch. It is likely that I did not know how to manage my affairs. There is nobody to teach me now how to mend my ways and start afresh. As if anyone could "start afresh" with nothing but a pack of claimants at his heels! I feel I must die so that you and my children may live in peace.'[14]

The letter is not signed, but the handwriting is clearly Kopp's and it was in his correspondence. It could have been a suicide note, but other letters follow after this date. The last in his hand dates from 5th May 1951, two months later. We can conclude he did not commit suicide. Kopp had an exuberant Russian character. Perhaps the letter reflects his moment of truth – he looked back and saw his splendid failures: his first marriage which yielded five healthy children, his Spanish adventure and the treason of his communist brothers in arms, his heroism in the Foreign Legion which nevertheless failed to stop the German fascists, his blurry espionage activities, and above all his financial muddles, which despite his creativity and capacity to work he could not solve. By writing this down, he was trying to exorcise his demons and to create a new perspective which would enable him to live on. It is not known if Doreen Hunton ever read this letter.

If hell is other people, then Kopp was in hell: in this case the Landron family and Mallier, the notary.[15] On 27th March he sent two letters from what was probably his last residence, namely La Provençale, Route de Salon, La Gavotte, Marseille. The first is addressed to Mr and Mrs Clayette-Landron. For professional reasons Kopp had to travel from here to there, so the Kopp-Hunton family, while waiting for the purchase of the estate, had rented a house from Juliette Landron and her husband Henry Clayette in Meung-sur-Loire. He asked them to make a balance for the rent and the costs he had incurred himself, such as for the installation of a boiler.

The second letter is addressed to Mallier. The tone is cold and hostile. He complains that, owing to his actions, Maxime Landron has turned out to be a tyrant and has seized Kopp's personal possessions. Kopp tries to intellectualize his arguments: '[…] and you now are trying to defend with sophisms […] Landron's blind brutality has no lack of a certain grandeur […] your attempt to intimidate my wife, whom you, in my absence, unjustly menaced with immediate expulsion.'

Two days later Kopp's life again took a more favourable turn. The French company Minerais & Minéraux Industriels was interested in Kopp's application of sieving and gravimetrical enrichment for the treatment of minerals.[16] The company granted him a credit of 30,000 French francs to manufacture a semi-industrial apparatus which could process minerals. They promised to consider the production of three other apparatuses. No design can be found of these. This seems to confirm the theory that the remaining plans and correspondence only constitute a fraction of the total documents. In his correspondence to his daughter Anne-Marie, for example, he writes about the production of agricultural machines, but this cannot be found in his archives.

In April 1951 he came into contact with the firm Olesen & Fetterlein again. The intermediary Rassow had apparently messed things up and his former contact Ivar Thomsen tried to get the production of the Tinto going again, and to negotiate with Olesen & Fetterlein and with Recks at the heater factory: 'It is not easy to get money out of people when everything looks pretty dark; therefore let us know how things stand and let us make a fresh start.'[17]

The last letter addressed to Kopp dates from 16th July 1951. The firm Minerais & Minéraux were enquiring about the plans for the apparatuses to process minerals, but Kopp had already died.

The very last letter in his correspondence dates from 15th October 1956. It concerns a request from his wife Doreen Hunton addressed to Messr. Wilkins, a manufacturer of washing machines. She asks whether the firm could not do anything with a design Kopp had made shortly before he died. There is a description of a washing machine 2129, dated 3rd January 1951.

The correspondence only partly reflects what has always been alleged. Kopp did get into financial trouble, but this is not solely due to his business venture with agricultural machines. His Tinto project and his megalomaniac attitude were also important causes. To buy a property like Brennes he needed a lot of money, but that money existed only virtually. When his manufacturers did not come through as generously as he had hoped, his projects collapsed like a house of cards.

What remains a mystery is the firm assertion of Kopp's children that their father returned to Paris after his financial debacle and worked as a consulting engineer for the company Société Générale

Nº 34

Transcription
de l'acte de Décès
de
KOPP
Georges.

Le quinze Juillet mil neuf cent cinquante un,
à dix sept heures est décédé 253 Avenue du
Prado ; Georges Kopp, né à Pétrograd (Russie)
le dix Juin mil neuf cent deux, ingénieur,
fils de .... époux de Thérèse Hunter,
domicilié les Cadeneaux, La Gavotte (B.d.R)
Dressé le seize Juillet mil neuf cent cinquante
un à quatorze heures trente sur la déclaration
de Douglas Bannett, Cinquante quatre ans
vice Consul d'Angleterre 1 rue d'Arcole,
Lecture faite. Nous Paul Catileon, Conseiller
Municipal Officier de l'Etat Civil, par
délégation avons signé avec lui.
Transcrit le vingt cinq Juillet mil neuf cent
Cinquante et un à quatorze heures par
Nous Odde Auguste Maire des Pennes-Mirabeau

de Pétroles Françaises, which later became the oil company Total. Michel and Anne-Marie met him there in 1950. That would explain why he went to Marseille, because the French oil terminal is there. But there are no written sources for this.

The death certificate does not lie. George Kopp died on 15th July 1951 at 5 o'clock in the afternoon at 253 Avenue du Prado, Pennes-Mirabeaux. The cause of death is not mentioned. The likely hypothesis is that his phlebitis of both legs created a blood clot in the bloodstream, which induced a pulmonary embolism leading to a heart attack. According to Anne-Marie, Doreen told her that he was repairing a clock when he died.

There is no trace of his grave.

EPILOGUE

By Professor Peter Davison

One of George Orwell's characteristics – and one not, of course, peculiar to him – was that he came to know many people in relationships that someone writing thirty, fifty or more years later may find difficult, even impossible, to pin down. Orwell seems to have kept his friends and acquaintance in near-watertight compartments. Those he knew well in one sphere of his life may not have been aware of those in other spheres. Many of those with whom he associated were significant in their time – David Astor, Max Plowman, Arthur Koestler, Cyril Connolly, for example – or, even if he did not know them personally but referred to them in his writing – Winston Churchill, Lenin, Francisco Largo Caballero – are easily traceable, so that some sort of biographical background can be sketched by an author or editor for his readers. However, there are inevitably those about whom we should like to know more. And that can also apply to places. No amount of digging has enabled me to discover why Orwell's first wife, Eileen, went to Chapel Ridding in Windermere in July 1938. The long letter she wrote from there to Jack Common hangs in a void.

But there is a yet more mysterious category. There are some few people whom we may think we have 'placed' but who have deceived us. They are enigmas. Of these Georges Kopp is, in Orwell's life, the most interesting, the most elusive, and the most intriguing. I must confess that at first I took him at face value and at his own estimation. I don't think I was seriously careless in so doing – one can always dig a little deeper about anyone; there is always more one can include in biographical footnotes – but there is also the imperative to be economical, not with the truth, but simply with the readers' patience.

For example, I have an interest in British Music Hall and hence was at first prepared to wax lyrical about Dan Leno. Very properly, one of my readers restrained me. Leno had little relevance to Orwell and I was guilty of indulging myself and boring those consulting the volumes whose chief interest was Orwell. Further, at some 8,500 pages, the twenty volumes I was preparing were demanding more of our forests than was easily justified. But Kopp was another matter. I did worry whether I should call him Georges or George, or even Jorge; after all, he himself used all three forms in quick succession. Initially I was content simply to reproduce his letters and reports (e.g., on Orwell's throat wound) and offer readers a very brief outline of his origins – that he was Russian by birth, Belgian by nationality, and Orwell's commander in Spain; that he was a civil engineer, 'but also something of an imposter' (*Complete Works*, vol. XI, 9). A longer note later in that volume (338–9) reproduces the account given in the *Independent News* 60, 23rd December 1938, describing Kopp's release from Franco's prisons, and that was prefaced by a note that 'The account given must have been derived from Kopp, who was not the most reliable of witnesses, but Orwell would have taken it at face value.' Later volumes reproduced what was readily then available – Kopp's settlement in England and Scotland, his marriage to Doreen Hunton (Orwell's wife's sister-in-law), the sale of a very dodgy truck to Orwell, and hints at Orwell's disenchantment with Kopp.

However, there was far more to Kopp than these brief notes indicated. When I produced *The Lost Orwell* in 2006, the supplementary volume to the *Complete Works*, I was fortunate in being permitted to include a short chapter (83–91) on further and much more significant revelations about Mr Kopp. These were generously given me by Mr Bert Govaerts of Antwerp and I was – and am – much indebted to him. All that Mr Govaerts passed to me is now fully amplified in this study. Furthermore, Kopp's story is illustrated by the very places where so much of the action took place. I hope it is not facetious to suggest that it all goes to provide a basis for a first-rate novel of the le Carré variety – but it is fact, so far as that can be ascertained.

One important aspect of the Kopp-Orwell-Eileen relationship does need to be stressed. This was revealed not by Mr Govaerts's research, but from letters which, coincidentally, I was able also to publish in

The Lost Orwell. One of the intriguing aspects was Kopp's relationship with Eileen Blair, Orwell's wife. To one biographer, D.J. Taylor, their relationship was 'one of the enigmas of the Orwells' Spanish trip'; to another, Gordon Bowker, it might have gone further, although had it done so, Orwell continued to hold Kopp 'in the highest regard' (*The Lost Orwell*, 83). However, now we know that Eileen was much more specific. Her husband, wrote Eileen to her close friend, Norah, had not noticed that Kopp was 'a bit gone on her', and, indeed, as she wrote, despite her feelings of guilt about their friendship, 'I wasn't what they call in love with Georges.' However, visiting Kopp in the disgusting prison in which he was held in Barcelona (something which put the Orwells in danger, of course), she could not bring herself to tell a man whom 'we were both confident' was about 'to be shot' that she was in no way in love with him. Then, as she put it so beautifully to her friend Norah, 'he has rotted in a filthy prison for more than six months with nothing to do but remember me in my most pliant moments' (71).

There is no doubt that Kopp was brave, but also no doubt that he was brilliant at embroidering his achievements. Nevertheless, so far as George Orwell was concerned, they each held a deep admiration for the other. Again to quote Eileen from that same letter, 'They went about saving each other's lives or trying to in a way that was almost horrible to me.' It is not clear whether Orwell ever really plumbed the depths of Kopp's deceptive behaviour. In a way that is surprising because he was one of the very few people, if not the only one, who suspected that Peter Smollett, as he was known in the United Kingdom – and to MI5 – was in fact Harry Peter Smolka, a KGB agent, codename 'Abo'. He was so successful that a grateful British government appointed him OBE (an officer of the Order of the British Empire) for his wartime services. And so successful was he in duping the British that the NKVD incorrectly thought British intelligence had turned him. Orwell, however, was not taken in: he had him down in his list of 'Fellow-Travellers' and 'Crypto-Communists'. Although Kopp is not in the same league as Smolka, it is an amusing sidelight to his deceptions that (as explained in Chapter 1), he claimed in questioning by MI5 that he 'did not want to be associated too closely with communism', little knowing (as did no one else at the time) that his MI5 handler, Anthony Blunt, was simultaneously a secret KGB agent! (See *The Lost Orwell*, 87, n.1.)

Despite being so perceptive over Smollett, Orwell never indicates that he was suspicious of the deceptions being practised by Kopp. Why was this? In part, of course, Orwell might well have valued the man's evident bravery and the care he took of him when he was wounded above Kopp's peccadilloes. Possibly, however, as a comrade-in-arms an accord was built up that counted for more than the norms of civilian life. Even in my extremely modest service in the armed forces from 1943 onwards, I can recognize that comradeship and loyalty in the forces can stand far above civilian norms. An almost insignificant example might illustrate this. While awaiting to be drafted to serve in the Far East in 1945 I was stationed at HMS Collingwood, a shore base near Portsmouth. At this base were half a dozen deserters who, under the eyes of the naval police and officers, lived on base and, quite literally, went out through perimeter fences each day to work in the city. No one thought of giving them away. Presumably in due course they moved on. Though they were not our specific comrades, they enjoyed a common lower-deck loyalty. Orwell, even if he realized that Kopp was not all that he said he was, would, I guess, have been bound by similar bonds of comradeship. What, after all, in those circumstances, was deceiving the authorities?

It may be that we shall never fully know all that Georges Kopp got up to, but we have here a fascinating account of a very intriguing man who, whatever his faults, was daring and courageous. For both we must be very grateful.

NOTES

Chapter 1: The Beginnings of a Turbulent Life

1 Alexander: born 21st September 1871. Guitalia: born 12th June 1876. Guitalia is the Russian diminutive of Guitle, which comes from the German Gut. She was the child of Anne Bermann and Michel Neimann.

2 The relatives in question are, among others, Georges Kopp's grandson Christopher Kopp and his youngest son, Quentin Kopp.

3 The growing anti-Semitism in Russia, especially the pogrom of 1905 in St Petersburg, may also be the cause of their sudden departure. However, Kopp's daughter has difficulties with this theory. According to Anne-Marie Kopp, her grandparents were certainly not religious Jews, since she has never seen any traces of any religion, let alone Jewish, in their home in Belgium. And she detected no anxiety about their Jewish descent from her grandmother during World War II. Her grandmother once told her a story which proves that they had Russian Orthodox icons in the ancestral house in Russia, and therefore it is unlikely that they were Jewish. Guitalia Neimann lived in the big family house with her grandmother. She always prayed in front of an icon, and the grandchildren, among others Guitalia, had placed a picture of their aunt in front of the icon. After a while her grandmother said, 'It is strange, but each time I pray, I think of your aunt.'

4 Immigration file 233, nr. 1149866; the family lived in Rue des Coteaux 233.

5 Archives, Marc Wildemeersch, thanks to Quentin Kopp.

6 Avenue Druez 19.

7 A firm making heaters and valves. MI5 file, 17th September 1943. Document reference HS 9/858/8. National Archives, London.

8 Rue de Vondel 6.

9 He was a sociologist who wrote several groundbreaking studies including one on bureaucracy, and eventually earned the position of director-general of the Ministry of Work.

10 Their children were, in order of birth: Michel (8th February 1926), Pierre (22nd October 1927), Jean (9th February 1929), Anne-Marie (6th July 1930) and Paul (26th January 1932).

11 It is essentially an order made by one person to another to pay money to a third person.

12 1 Belgian franc of 1936 is worth 30.84 francs in 2010, a euro is worth 40.3399 francs (source: National Bank of Belgium and FOD Economics and Energy).

13 Copy archives, Marc Wildemeersch.

14 MI5 file, 17th September 1943.

15 It is ironic that he did not want to reveal his possible links with the Left, when his handler at M15 was Anthony Blunt, a KGB agent and communist, as will be explained in later chapters.

16 Interview with Anne-Marie Kopp, 21st February 2000, recorded in Genval. Personal archives, Marc Wildemeersch.

Chapter 2: 'A Comic Opera with an Occasional Death'

1 A. Beevor, *The Battle for Spain* (London: Weidenfeld & Nicolson, 2006), xxxi.

2 J. Sommerfield, *Vrijwilliger in Spanje: Oorlogsdomein* (Amsterdam: Knack, 2008), 115. Translated from Dutch.

3 A. Helman, *De sfinx van Spanje* (De Bilt: Uitgeverij Schokland, 2011), 99.

4 Sommerfield, *Vrijwilliger in Spanje*, 34. Translated from Dutch.

5 Ibid., 170. Translated from Dutch.

6 E. Hemingway, 'Under the Ridge'. Online: http://pdbooks.ca/books/english/authors/hemingway-ernest/short-stories/part-two/under-the-ridge.html (accessed 7th August 2013).

7 Beevor, *The Battle for Spain*, 428.

8 Archives of the Aliens Police (Aliens Office), Brussels, file 233, nr.1149866.

9 R. Stradling, 'The Spies Who Loved Them: The Blairs in Barcelona, 1937', *Intelligence and National Security* 25:5 (October 2010): 638–55.

10 Six according to Anne-Marie Kopp, his daughter. Eight according to Doreen Hunton, Kopp's second wife.

11 G. Orwell, *Homage to Catalonia* (London: Penguin Classics, 2000), 11.

12 'Un rescape de geôles staliniennes, Georges Kopp', *L'Espagne Nouvelle*, Année III, nr. 61, 15th January 1939; *Independent News*, no. 60, 23rd December 1938.

13 A. Durgan, *Revolutionary History: The Spanish Civil War: The View from the Left* (London: Socialist Platform, 1992), 291. See also: Andy Durgan, 'International Volunteers in the POUM Militias', Libcom.org. Online: http://libcom.org/history/international-volunteers-poum-militias (accessed 7th August 2013).

14 Miguel Pedrola was a member of the POUM youth organization killed in action near Huesca in 1936.

15 A party from the Left with a strong pacifist and international character. You could situate the ILP between Labour and the communists.

16 H.E. Kaminski, *Ceux de Barcelone* (Paris: Denoël, 1937; reprinted – Paris: Editions Allia, 2003).

17 Orwell, *Homage*, 136.

18 See C. Hall, *'Not Just Orwell': The Independent Labour Party Volunteers and the Spanish Civil War* (Barcelona: Warren & Pell Publishing), 116, 146.

19 Helman, *De sfinx van Spanje*, 59. Helman also calls the POUM a small but influential and intelligent party.

20 As told by Victor Pardo, head of the documentation centre on the civil war, situated in Robres. The bullet holes can still be seen.

21 Photograph by the author, 2011. Located by Victor Pardo. The buildings are now empty.

22 Photograph by the author, 2011. Located by Victor Pardo.

23 Orwell, *Homage*, 17.

24 Ibid., 32.

25 Ibid., 85.

26 J. Pané, 'Gregorio Jorge, l'heroi desconegut', Fundación Andreu Nin website. Online: http://www.fundanin.org/pane.htm (accessed 9 July 2013).

27 Ibid.

28 The *New Leader* was the official newspaper of the ILP.

29 The quote comes from the poet Robert Burns.

30 Orwell, *Homage*, 23.

31 Ibid., 22.

32 Ibid., 189.

33 In his letters describing military actions Kopp regularly mentions members of the ILP, so we can assume that Kopp was in the neighbourhood of the contingent. Orwell first called Monte Irazo 'Monte Oscure', realized his mistake and changed it to Monte Trazo, but the real name is Monte Irazo. The Ruta de Orwell, some reconstructed trenches, are situated on the Monte Irazo, according to Victor Pardo. The two positions were closer to one another than that Orwell remembered.

34 The *New Leader*, 5th March 1937.

35 Orwell, *Homage*, 39.

36 According to Victor Pardo, who was surveying the reconstruction of some of the trenches of the Ruta de Orwell.

37 'All Quiet on the Monte Irazo Front' is a pun on *All Quiet on the Western Front*, a classic novel on World War I by Erich Maria Remarque.

38 See map below.

39 Benjamin Levinski, second in command after Kopp.

40 Orwell, *Homage*, 59.

41 Ibid., 49.

42 *Plano de Communicaciones, Aragon*, Comite de Defensa, Barbastro, 29th November 1936. Documentation Centre, Robres.

43 Photograph by the author, 9 July 2011.

44 Several sources mention different dates for her arrival.

45 Again several dates circulate. Orwell himself situates his injury towards the end of March, and she visited him during the ten days he spent in hospital. The photograph of Eileen and Orwell at the front is dated 13th March 1937.

46 G. Bowker, *George Orwell* (London: Little, Brown, 2003), 211.

47   Orwell, *Homage*, 63–4.
48   Gregorio Jorge, battalion commander and Kopp's good friend.
49   D. Bateman, 'Georges Kopp and the POUM Militia', Marxists.org. Online:
     http://www.marxists.org/history/etol/revhist/backiss/vol4/no1-2/kopp.
     htm (accessed 9th July 2013).
50   S. Wadhams, *Remembering Orwell* (Harmondsworth: Penguin, 1984), 82. Harry
     Milton's real name was Wolf Kupinski. It is likely but not certain that he was
     speaking about the raid on Ermita Salas.
51   After the May events, Kopp left the POUM. This will be discussed in the
     next chapters. The International Brigades were units made up of volunteers
     from different countries to defend the Republic. From 1937 on they were
     controlled by the Stalinist communists.
52   Mentioned on a document of the Foreign Legion, copy archives, Marc
     Wildemeersch.
53   Josep Pané, 'Gregorio Jorge'.
54   P. Davison, (Red.). *The Lost Orwell* (London: Timewell Press, 2006), photo no. 8:
     'The Firing Line'. Davison does not mention Kopp, but he acknowledges in
     an email to the author that it could be him.
55   An NPO dedicated to the POUM: http://www.fundanin.org

Chapter 3: On Heroism and Banality

1   The anarchists belonged to the CNT: Confederación Nacional del Trabajo.
2   NKVD: Narodnyi Kommissariat Vnutrennich Del. SIM: Servicio de
    Investigación Militar.
3   The assault guards would be either *guardias de asalto* (local or of Valencia) or
    guardias civiles. Orwell, too, confused them constantly. Both were mistrusted by
    the Left.
4   Photo by the author, 2008.
5   Other sources mention 27th April.
6   Photo: author, 2011.
7   Orwell merely mentions 'an American', but Milton confirmed that he was
    that American. C. Hall, *Not Just Orwell* (Barcelona: Warren & Pell, 2009), 216.
8   G. Orwell, *Homage to Catalonia* (London: Penguin Classics, 2000), 109.
9   Photo: author, 2008.
10 Photo: author, 2008.
11 Orwell, *Homage*, 116.
12 Ibid., 111.
13 Ibid., 118.
14 Ibid., 124.
15 Photo: author, 2011.
16 Orwell, *Homage*, 137.
17 G. Bowker, *George Orwell* (London: Little, Brown, 2003), 221.

18 Orwell archives; and collection, Bert Govaerts.

19 P. Davison, ed., *Orwell in Spain* (London: Penguin: 2001), 123–5.

20 A. Durgan, 'International Volunteers in the POUM Militias', Libcom.org. Online: http://libcom.org/history/international-volunteers-poum-militias (accessed 7th August 2013).

21 Orwell, *Homage*, 153.

22 Ibid., 154.

23 J. McNair, *Spanish Diary* (Manchester: Greater Manchester ILP, 1979), 25.

24 R. Stradling, 'The Spies Who Loved Them: The Blairs in Barcelona, 1937', *Intelligence and National Security* 25:5 (October 2010): line 595 and note 45.

25 See Chapter 5.

26 He certainly knew it later, see Chapter 5.

Chapter 4: The Revolution Eats Its Children

1 Robert Smillie is mentioned again in Chapter 6.

2 D. Murray, the *New Leader*, 13th August 1937. David Murray was an ILP member, a businessman and a friend of Bob Smillie's family, and he was sent to Valencia to help him. He said that Smillie's death was accidental due to peritonitis.

3 G. Orwell, *Homage to Catalonia* (London: Penguin Classics, 2000), 171–3.

4 Ibid., 175.

5 P. Davison, ed., *Complete Works of George Orwell*, 2nd edition, vol. XI (London: Secker and Warburg, 1998), 30.

6 G. Bowker, *George Orwell* (London: Little, Brown, 2003), 227.

7 Orwell, *Homage*, 116.

8 Tioli worked as a spy for the PSUC. He spied on the Blairs and Georges Kopp. See R. Stradling, 'The Spies Who Loved Them', *Intelligence and National Security* 25:5 (October 2010) 651–4.

9 P. Davison, ed., *Complete Works*, 49.

10 B. Govaerts, 'George Kopp: De vreemde voetnoot in een beroemd leven', *Vrij Nederland*, 24 August 1985, 11.

11 Alexander was the father of Bob Smillie, who fought with Kopp.

12 J. Meyers, 'Repeating the Old Lies', *The New Criterion* (April 1999). Online: http://orwell.ru/a_life/Spanish_War/english/e_olies (accessed 7 August 2013).

13 D. Crook, *Hampstead Heath to Tian An Men: The Autobiography of David Crook*. Online: http://davidcrook.net/simple/chapter4.html (accessed 10th July 2013).

14 The NKVD planned to liquidate the POUM as early as October 1936. Victor Orlov, head of NKVD, gave Stalin that assurance. P. Davison, *Complete Works*, vol. XI, 32 in the revised text.

15 B. Crick, *George Orwell: A Life* (London: Little, Brown, 1985), 231–2.

16 G. Mak, *In Europa: Reizen door de twintigste eeuw* (Amsterdam: Atlas, 2004), 399.

17 Kopp himself used the abbreviation GPU or GPOU, the forerunner of the NKVD, when referring to the Russian secret police.

18 Author unknown, 'Un rescape de geôles staliniennes, Georges Kopp', *L'Espagne Nouvelle*, année III, nr. 61, 15th January 1939.
19 P. Davison, ed., *The Lost Orwell* (London: Timewell Press, 2006).
20 Campo de Trabajo is not mentioned in the article in *L'Espagne Nouvelle*.
21 Alien file 233, nr. 1149866.
22 R. Stradling, 'The Spies Who Loved Them', *Intelligence and National Security* 25:5 (October 2010): 650–51.

Chapter 5: Wein, Weib und Gesang

1 Waltz of Johan Straus II, symbol of a hedonistic lifestyle.
2 D.J. Taylor, 'Another Piece of the Puzzle', *Guardian*, 10th Dec 2005. Online: http://www.guardian.co.uk/books/2005/dec/10/georgeorwell.classics (accessed 10 July 2013).
3 P. Davison, *The Lost Orwell* (London: Timewell Press, 2006), 64.
4 Taylor, 'Another Piece of the Puzzle'.
5 G. Bowker, *George Orwell* (London: Little, Brown, 2003), 247.
6 Davison, *The Lost Orwell*, 71–2.
7 Ibid.
8 Ibid.
9 Ibid.
10 Bowker, *George Orwell*, 214.
11 Ibid.
12 R. Stradling, 'The Spies Who Loved Them', *Intelligence and National Security* 25:5 (October 2010), 647. Crook and Tioli will be mentioned later.
13 Bowker, *George Orwell*, 219ff. This information was meant to blackmail them if necessary.
14 Stradling, 'The Spies Who Loved Them', 648.

Chapter 6: Free at Last

1 MI5 file, document reference HS 9/858/8, National Archives, London.
2 G. Cohen, *The Failure of a Dream: The Independent Labour Party from Disaffiliation to World War II* (London: Tauris, 2007), 187–8.
3 Orwell Archives, University College London.
4 Mark Rafailovich Rein was born in 1909 in Vilnius, Lithuania. In 1936 he went to Spain to support the Republican government during the Spanish Civil War. On 9th April 1937 he was kidnapped in Barcelona by Russian agents. The intention was to use him in the show trial of Rykov and Bukharin in the USSR. In spite of numerous efforts by his father, Rafail Abramovich, and Western socialist supporters, no one ever saw him alive, so it is presumed that he was murdered (http://en.wikipedia.org/wiki/Mark_Rein – accessed 7 August 2013). Gaston Weil probably died in prison because of neglect and disease.

A militiaman, he was imprisoned on suspicion of being responsible for the squandering of his battalion's funds. Georges Chenais was a commercial trader who was arrested and went missing during his stay in a Spanish prison. His fate is unknown.

5 30th January 1939, Letters of Georges Kopp, George Orwell Archive, University College London, folio 1.

6 Ibid., folio 4.

7 J. Newsinger, 'The Death of Bob Smillie', *The Historical Journal* 41:2 (1998): 575.

8 T. Buchanan, 'The Death of Bob Smillie: A Reply', *The Historical Journal* 43:4 (2000): 1109–12.

9 M. Shelden, *Orwell: The Authorised Biography* (New York/London: Harper Collins, 1991).

10 Some sources mention Toulon.

11 In his file on Marc Rein dated 9th January he writes that he had been in Brussels ten days before.

12 Recorded conversation with the author, 21st February 2007, Genval, Belgium.

13 George Orwell Archive, University College London.

14 Ibid.

15 Peter Davison, *The Lost Orwell* (London: Timewell Press, 2006), 75–6.

16 In his MI5 file it says he arrived in March 1938.

17 George Orwell Archive, University College London.

18 Ibid. Translation from French: 'Small essay on the Marxist analysis of the events in Spain 1936–1939'.

19 Ibid., 2.

20 Ibid., 11.

21 Historical materialism is based on the theory of Karl Marx (1818–83). It states that all form of social thoughts such as art or family develop on an economic base. They are altered as a result of class struggle. Each ruling class destroys or replaces the other. The aim is to produce a classless society thus reducing the economy to a less important factor (http://dictionary.reference.com/browse/ historical+materialism / https://en.wikipedia.org/wiki/Historical_materialism– accessed 7 August 2013).

Chapter 7: 'I Want to Live Grand and Gloriously'

1 Hendrik Marsman, 'De grijsaard en de jongeling'. In translation: 'The old man and the youth'.

2 The Maginot Line was a line of concrete fortifications, and other defences such as machine guns posts which France constructed along its borders to stop a German invasion (http://www.historylearningsite.co.uk/maginot_line.htm – accessed 7 August 2013).

3 'George and Evelyn' were most probably George and Evelyn Mason. George, a thoracic surgeon, was a medical colleague of Laurence O'Shaughnessy.
4 MI5 file, 17 December 1941, document reference HS 9/858/8, National Archives, London.
5 A complex network of nerves located in the abdomen.
6 Doreen Hunton, his wife, received this pension from the French government until her death in 1969.
7 B. Govaerts, 'Comandante Georges Kopp 1902–1953: De Belgische vriend van George Orwell', *Brood en Rozen* 2 (2007): 20.

Chapter 8: In Service of a Puppet Government

1 In the 1930s, Dr Hermann Zorn of I.G. Farben Industries in Germany began to search for lubricants with the properties of natural oils but without the tendencies to gel or gum when used in an engine environment. His work led to the preparation of over 3,500 esters in the late 1930s and early 1940s, including diester, polyolester and banana oil. During the same time period in the United States, Dr William Albert Zismann, working at the US Naval Research Laboratory (NRL), was also synthesizing esters, especially diester. Through the 1930s, Standard Oil of Indiana was also working on the extraction of synthetic feedstocks from animal fat and plant seed oil.
2 MI5 file, 17 December 1941, document reference HS 9/858/8, National Archives, London.
3 Ibid.
4 In 1960 the French franc had a value of 100 old francs. So 500,000 is equivalent to 5000 new French francs. Not taking into account inflation and price evolutions, a euro is worth 6.55957 French francs.
5 MI5 file, document reference HS 9/858/8.
6 Ibid.
7 Ibid.
8 Ibid.
9 Special Operations Executive.
10 6328 is the reference number assigned to Kopp.
11 Ibid.
12 Ibid.
13 'Sd' stands for *soldat* (i.e., soldier).
14 Courtesy Bert Govaerts, SOMA/AA 1333/Sûreté d'État.
15 MI5 file, document reference HS 9/858/8.
16 Ibid.
17 Ibid.
18 Rexism was a fascist political movement in the first half of the twentieth century in Belgium. It was the ideology of the Rexist Party (Parti Rexiste), officially called Rex, founded in 1930 by Léon Degrelle, a Walloon.

19 MI5 file, document reference HS 9/858/8.
20 Alien file 233 nr. 1149866.
21 Ibid.
22 V. Alba and S. Schwartz, *Spanish Marxism versus Soviet Communism: A History of the P.O.U.M. in the Spanish Civil War* (New Brunswick: Transaction Publishers, 2009), 154.
23 MI5 file, document reference HS 9/858/8.
24 B. Govaerts, 'Comandante Georges Kopp 1902–1953: De Belgische vriend van George Orwell', *Brood en Rozen* 2 (2007): 2.

Chapter 9: Spy... or Double Spy?

 1 MI5 file, 17 December 1941, document reference HS 9/858/8, National Archives, London.
 2 Kopp had probably mentioned his mother's death in previous letters, but wouldn't have known which letters had reached them.
 3 MI5 file document reference HS 9/858/8.
 4 Doreen Hunton, Gwen O'Shaughnessy, and George and Evelyn Mason.
 5 MI5 file document reference HS 9/858/8.
 6 Ibid.
 7 MI5 file document reference HS 9/858/8. 'Guepeou' refers to the Russian secret police.
 8 Quentin Kopp is the second son of Doreen Hunton and Georges and the seventh of the two marriages. In February 2007 I interviewed him in Dunkirk and stayed with him from 11th to 13th April in Pilsley near Chesterfield. There I could consult all the sources related to his father.
 9 Doreen Hunton died on 30th July 1969.
10 Email to the author, 24th February 2007.
11 Email to the author, 26th February 2007.
12 Copy archives, Marc Wildemeersch. The Aliens Order Registration Certificate is a sort of identity card for foreigners residing in Great Britain.
13 Photo courtesy of Quentin Kopp.

Chapter 10: Gentleman, Farmer, Inventor

 1 MI5 file, document reference HS 9/858/8.
 2 Ibid.
 3 Ibid.
 4 Ibid.
 5 Richard Blair and Quentin Kopp have remained good friends till now. From left to right Richard Blair, Quentin Kopp and their respective wives on a trip to visit where their fathers fought in Spain.

6   *Hysterion* is Greek for uterus, an illustration of her black humour.
7   Quoted in Rosemary Haskell, 'The Pain of Being Ill and Uncovered', Newsobserver.com, 5th July 2009. Online: http://www.newsobserver. com/2009/07/05/76218/the-pain-of-being-ill-and-uncovered.html (accessed 7 August 2013).
8   'Is This Where Orwell Created Big Brother?' *Northern Echo*, 23rd June 2003. Online: http://www.thenorthernecho.co.uk/archive/2003/06/23/7026248. Is_this_where_Orwell_created_Big_Brother_/ (accessed 13th June 2013).
9   Email to the author, 26th February 2007.
10 Mary Wheeler, in conversation with the author, 12th April 2007.
11 Archives, Marc Wildemeersch. The Belgian Brigade in the email refers to the Brigade Piron. The unit consisted of two thousand soldiers under British command who had fled from Belgium and Luxembourg.
12 Archives, Marc Wildemeersch.
13 Email to the author, 26th February 2007.
14 Photo archives, Quentin Kopp.
15 Correspondence archives, Marc Wildemeersch, courtesy of Quentin Kopp.

Chapter 11: To Be or Not to Be O'Brien

1   J. Meyers, *Wintry Conscience of a Generation* (New York: Norton, 2000), 260.
2   Email to the author, 26th February 2007.
3   G. Orwell, *Nineteen Eighty-Four*, Part 3, Chapter 3. Online: http:// ebooks.adelaide.edu.au/o/orwell/george/o79n/chapter3.3.html (accessed 13th July 2013).

4 Ibid., Part 3, Chapter 2. Online: http://ebooks.adelaide.edu.au/o/orwell/
   george/o79n/chapter3.2.html (accessed 13th July 2013).
5 This is an old English song often sung by soldiers, boy scouts and rugby
   players, popular at the time he wrote *Homage*.
6 G. Orwell, *Homage to Catalonia* (London: Penguin Classics, 2000), 54.
7 Ibid, 81.
8 Ibid, 59.

Chapter 12: Downhill

1 Anne-Marie Kopp, recorded conversation with the author, Genval,
   21st February 2007. She refers to letters her father wrote.
2 Email to the author, 13th February 2007, and archives Bert Govaerts.
3 It was clear that many of his inventions were too far ahead their time, since
   they have subsequently enjoyed great success in diverse fields. Coal-cutting
   technology based on the same concepts was universally used by the UK's
   National Coal Board. The baby buggy has been marketed successfully for
   many years by the Maclaren company among others. An almost identically
   designed washing machine to the one he created was made by Philips from
   the 1970s onwards. Courtesy of Quentin Kopp.
4 The name refers to a hill which lies opposite the still-intact estate of Toftcombs
   House.
5 Copies archives, Marc Wildemeersch, originals in possession of Quentin Kopp.
6 The principle used was that of drip-feeding the oil. This became a common
   form of heating until the 1970s, when central heating became more widely
   used in the UK as gas became available from the North Sea. Courtesy of
   Quentin Kopp.
7 Ibid.
8 Ibid.
9 Courtesy of Quentin Kopp. Whaley Bridge is on the A6, which in those
   days was the main road from London to Manchester, and is also on a
   railway line to Manchester, which is only a few miles away. It is also only
   about fifty kilometres from Sheffield and about one hundred kilometres from
   Birmingham.
10 Quentin Kopp: 'My Mother always had a dim view of "Sunday" Christians.
   The person who deceived him was a prominent member of one of the
   protestant churches (not the Church of England) who practised unchristian
   ethics during the week.'
11 For her 'clerical job', she worked for John A.F. Watson, who was senior
   chairman of the Juvenile Courts for the Inner London area. Courtesy of
   Quentin Kopp.
12 1,100,000 old French francs becomes 11,000 new French francs. Taking into
   account several parameters such as inflation, this has to be multiplied by
   7,700 francs, which is equivalent to 11,738 euros.

13 Copies archives, Marc Wildemeersch, originals in possession of Quentin Kopp.
14 Ibid.
15 'L'enfer, c'est les autres' (J.P. Sartre).
16 The Oxford English Dictionary defines gravimetric analysis as a quantitative chemical analysis based on the weighing of reagents and products.
17 Copies archives, Marc Wildemeersch, originals in possession of Quentin Kopp.

SOURCES

Archives:

Archives of the Aliens Police (Aliens Office), Brussels, file 233, nr. 1149866.
British Library, London, manuscript 49384.
Documentation centre, Robres, Spain (Victor Pardo).
Marc Wildemeersch archive: copies of photos, letters and documents of Georges Kopp in possession of Quentin, Anne-Marie and Michel Kopp.
National Archives, London, document reference HS 9/858/8.
Orwell Archive, University College London.

Books:

Alba, V. and S. Schwartz. *Spanish Marxism versus Soviet Communism: A History of the P.O.U.M. in the Spanish Civil War* (New Brunswick: Transaction Publishers, 2009).

Beevor, A. *The Battle for Spain.* London: Weidenfeld & Nicolson, 2006.

Bowker, G. *George Orwell.* London: Little, Brown, 2003.

Crick, B. *George Orwell: A Life.* London: Little, Brown, 1985.

Daane, M. *Het spoor van Orwell.* Amsterdam-Antwerpen: Atlas, 2011.

Davison, P., ed. *The Complete Works of George Orwell.* London: Secker and Warburg, 1998.

_____, ed. *Orwell in Spain.* London: Penguin, 2001.

_____, ed. *The Lost Orwell.* London: Timewell Press, 2006.

Hall, C. *Not Just Orwell.* Barcelona: Warren & Pell, 2009.

_____. *In Spain with Orwell.* Perth: Tippermuir Books, 2013.

Helman, A. *Sfinx van Spanje.* De Bilt: Uitgeverij Schokland, 2011.

Hemingway, E. *Verhalen uit de Spaanse Burgeroorlog.* Amsterdam: Contact, 1972.

Kaminski, H.E. *Ceux de Barcelone* (Paris: Editions Allia, 2003).

Lewis, P. *The Road to 1984.* London: Heinemann/Quixote Press, 1981.

Mak, G. *In Europa: Reizen door de twintigste eeuw*, 13th edition. Amsterdam: Atlas, 2004.

Meyers, J. *Wintry Conscience of a Generation.* New York: Norton, 2000.

Mitchell, D. *De Spaanse Burgeroorlog-Ooggetuigen spreken na de dood van Franco.* Weesp: Het Wereldvenster, 1986.

McNair, J. *Spanish Diary* (Manchester: Greater Manchester ILP, 1979).

Orwell, G. *Homage to Catalonia*. London: Penguin Classics, 2000.
Shelden, M. *Orwell: The Authorised Biography*. New York/London: Collins, 1991.
Sommerfield, J. *Vrijwilliger in Spanje*. Knack, 2008.
Van Belle, J. *Die lange hete zomer*. Zedelgem: Uitgeverij Flandria Nostra, 2008.
Wadhams, S. *Remembering Orwell* (Harmondsworth: Penguin, 1984).

Articles in Magazines:

Buchanan, T. 'The Death of Bob Smillie: A Reply'. *The Historical Journal* 43: 4 (2000): 1109–12.
Edwards, B. 'Soldier of Socialism'. *New Leader*, 13th August 1937, 2.
Govaerts, B. 'Comandante Georges Kopp 1902–1953: De Belgische vriend van George Orwell'. *Brood en Rozen* 2 (2007): 5–21.
Govaerts, B. 'George Kopp: De vreemde voetnoot in een beroemd leven'. *Vrij Nederland*, vol. 46, 24 August 1985, 11.
Kopp, A-M. 'Reactie op de bijdrage van Bert Govaerts'. *Brood en Rozen* 1 (2008): 84–7.
L'Espagne Nouvelle. 'Un rescape de geôles staliniennes, Georges Kopp'. Ann. III, n. 61, 15th January 1939.
Murray, D. 'Georges Kopp's Arrest'. *New Leader*, 13th August 1937, 2.
Newsinger, J. 'The Death of Bob Smillie'. *The Historical Journal* 41:2 (1998): 575.
Stradling, R. 'The Spies Who Loved Them'. *Intelligence and National Security* 25:5 (October 2010): 638–55.

Internet:

'Is This Where Orwell Created Big Brother?' *Northern Echo*, 23rd June 2003. Online: http://www.thenorthernecho.co.uk/archive/2003/06/23/7026248.Is_this_where_Orwell_created_Big_Brother_/ (accessed 13th June 2013).
Bateman, B. 'Georges Kopp and the POUM Militia'. Marxists.org. Online: http://www.marxists.org/history/etol/revhist/backiss/vol4/no1-2/kopp.htm (accessed 9th July 2013).
Crook, D. *Hampstead Heath to Tian An Men: The Autobiography of David Crook*. Online: http://davidcrook.net/simple/chapter4.html (accessed 10th July 2013).
Durgan, Andy. 'International Volunteers in the POUM Militias'. Libcom.org. Online: http://libcom.org/history/international-volunteers-poum-militias (accessed 7th August 2013).
Meyers, Jeffrey. 'Repeating the Old Lies', *The New Criterion* (April 1999). Online: http://orwell.ru/a_life/Spanish_War/english/e_olies (accessed 7 August 2013).
Orwell, G. *Nineteen Eighty-Four*. Online: http://ebooks.adelaide.edu.au/o/orwell/george/o79n/chapter3.3.html (accessed 13th July 2013).

Pané, J. 'Gregorio Jorge, l'heroi desconegut'. Fundación Andreu Nin website. Online: http://www.fundanin.org/pane.htm (accessed 9th July 2013).

Taylor, D.J. 'Another Piece of the Puzzle'. *Guardian*, 10th Dec 2005. Online: http://www.guardian.co.uk/books/2005/dec/10/georgeorwell.classics (accessed 10 July 2013).

ACKNOWLEDGEMENTS

The cliché says that the way to your goal is more important than the goal itself. This may be true, but who does not want something to show for it? The persons listed below helped me in my quest to understand Georges Kopp and with the realization of this biography.

Without Allan Warren's enthusiastic help this extensive and revised English version of *De man die Belg wilde worden: Georges Kopp, commandant van George Orwell* would not have been realized. He and Victor Pardo guided me around the battle scene in Aragon, and he helped me to visualize Orwell's actions in Barcelona.

Bert Govaerts began the scientific, historical approach to Georges Kopp and inspired me to deepen the subject. He showed me that working with primary sources is a must. Professor Peter Davison, the authority on Orwell, provided the epilogue and was always very supportive from our first contact onwards. Gordon Bowker, eminent historian, encouraged me to make an English version of my Dutch book. Tom Buchanan, lecturer at the University of Oxford, and Christopher Hall, author of *Not Just Orwell*, kindly helped me during my search. During my stay in Barcelona in July 2011 both Andy Durgan and Nick Lloyd, experts on the Barcelona scene during the Spanish Civil War, agreed to see me and helped me out. David Milton, the son of Harry, kindly forwarded some of his father's letters.

Without the collaboration of Quentin Kopp, the youngest son of Georges Kopp, I would not have succeeded in gaining an insight into the final phase of my protagonist's life. I was welcomed to stay with him in Pilsley several times. He helped me to access all the primary and secondary sources that were within his reach without any inclination to change my views on his father. He brought me into contact with numerous people who could help me further when I got stuck. Anne-Marie Kopp, Georges's oldest daughter, received me most hospitably in her house in Genval. It must not be easy to share the legacy of your father with historians. Furthermore, Michel Kopp, Georges's oldest son, and Christophe Kopp, his grandchild, kindly answered my numerous questions.

I thank my wife Ellen, my children Bastiaan, Korneel, Jasmien and my youngest son Briek because they kept on believing in this project when many others did not.

www.ingramcontent.com/pod-product-compliance
Lightning Source LLC
Jackson TN
JSHW020021141224
75386JS00025B/637